Tree Tips & Forest Facts: Essays on Living in and Sustaining California's Forests

First printed in September 2003 in Ukiah, California.

Text and photos: Claralynn R. Nunamaker, Registered Professional Forester #2606

First printing by FIRS, Forestry Information, Information & Services, Redwood Valley, California

Front cover: Snag overlooking the hills of south of Willits, California.

This book is dedicated to the forest landowners of the state of California who are working hard to ensure that our state's forests will remain as viable, functioning, intact forests for future generations.

Foreword

This book is a collection of many of the weekly articles that appeared between December 1998 and September 2003 as the *Tree Tips & Forest Facts* column in the Mendocino County Observer. A few edits have been made, but the essays are substantially the same as those that originally appeared in the Observer. Additionally, where I have color photos, these replace their black-and-white predecessors.

Since this book was first published in 2003, much has changed, yet much has stayed the same. One thing that has changed is that the column no longer runs. Once I moved to Scotland, fellow forester Thembi Borras penned the column for a time. When she moved on, sadly, the column ended. What remains constant are principles of forest ecology and sustainable land management. Here in Scotland for example, I've found that while the specifics of species and climate are different, general principles of sound management reflect what I learned through years in the field in California.

Through these pages, I aim to share some of that knowledge and those experiences with you. To the extent it helps you improve your understanding, appreciation, and enjoyment of the forests near you, this book will have served its purpose..

Claralynn 'Clare' Nunamaker
24 December 2012
Forres, Scotland

Over the last fifteen years I have worked as a forester in many capacities -- with the Forest Service, with a private consulting firm, as a freelance consultant helping individual landowners, and contracting with SmartWood to assess forests and foresters in the US and China for their commitment to sustainability. In all these roles, I've often heard and sometimes heard myself say the mantra, "They just don't understand."

While studying at Humboldt State University for masters degrees in both Forestry and Environmental Systems, we learned, predictably, that we need natural resource managers who understand forest ecology and management. But we also learned that the role of everyday people and communities is critical in developing sustainable forests. We are seeing that played out in California's forests today.

It seemed that instead of arguing over who is right and who is wrong, the emphasis ought to be on providing information that can enable people to make wise decisions for themselves and, if they are forest landowners, for their forests. It is the purpose of *Tree Tips and Forest Facts* to do just that.

Clare Nunamaker is a Registered Professional Forester (RPF) living in Mendocino County, California.

This book is not intended to be a comprehensive discussion of all aspects of forest ecology and forest management. You will find gaps, and you may find yourself challenging my interpretations of certain topics. Please take what you find helpful and leave what is not. If you're so moved, please write me at *forestry@nunamaker.com*. And may we all direct our energies towards improving the health of our forests in California and beyond.

Acknowledgements

In late 1998, while working as a "dirt" field forester in Laytonville, California I approached the editor of the local paper with an idea for a weekly forestry column. "Send it on in," was the reply, and so Jim Shields began running *Tree Tips & Forest Facts* each week in the Mendocino County Observer.

In 2001, a forest landowner by the name of Don Morosi who had regularly read the column for several years called up to say, "You have got to get this information to more people. Put those columns into a book." Two years later he called again, repeated his message, and said wouldn't let up this time until it was done. I believed him. Thanks, Don, for the push.

Many of the ideas presented in these pages coalesced over discussions on the long drives to and from the field during the years when I worked with fellow forester Brian Talbert. An excellent and thoughtful forester full of intriguing ideas and unique ways of expressing them, Brian will recognize in this book many of his ideas that we talked about in the truck as the miles of forest rolled by.

The number of forestry professionals to thank are far too many to list here, but Dick Priddy of Happy Camp, California merits special mention, as do Bill Dann, Jim Hawkins, Zhu Zhaohua, Zeng Yanru, Lu Wenming, Bill Keye, and Gary Nakamura. The Institute for Sustainable Forestry, the Forestry Institute for Teachers, and the Redwood Valley Outdoor Education Project also deserve special mention for the ways in which they have contributed to the content of these essays.

Living examples of forestland stewards I have had the pleasure of working with and learning from include Barbara Baxter, Steve Brown, Chris Hayes, Dave Herman and Jim Greig of Redtree Properties, Ed Tunheim, and so many more. Once again, thanks to Don and Nina Morosi for your support and encouragement in developing this book.

Special thanks go to Mendocino County Observer editors Jim & Susan Shields for giving *Tree Tips & Forest Facts* its start.

For that personal support that we all must have to sustain our efforts, thanks to Nancy Gallop, Sunny & Willard Bristol, John Renbourn, and, of course and as always, Grandma.

Part I -- Understanding the Forest

The Ecosystem Level

<u>Chaos in the Forest</u>

One of my college professors was fond of repeatedly reminding us that everywhere in the forest what you find is chaos. Overstory canopy cover? Chaos. Snag distribution? Chaos. Tree regeneration? Chaos. What he was teaching us is that we might understand the scientific principles behind the mechanics of how trees grow or a forest ecosystem functions, but when it comes to individual plants or animals, exactly how or where something will grow or thrive is unpredictable and sometimes surprising. Chaos, in fact.

You might accurately predict, for example, that there will be a fire of a certain size on average once every 20 years. You may even be able to predict which hillsides are most likely to burn. But you can't predict when the fire will start or how many trees it will damage and kill.

You might also accurately predict that a forest of young trees will grow and have a certain average height, diameter, and volume by a certain age. But you can't predict that a specific tree will be so many feet tall in a certain number of years. The tree might be killed by competition, browsed on heavily by deer, or have its top broken in a windstorm.

Overlooking the mountains between Ukiah and Willits in northern California.

Or you might predict that in a certain kind of stand, a specific type of mammal or bird will make its home. But you don't know where exactly it will make its nest or den, and you don't know where its favorite foraging spots will be.

What is the purpose in having an understanding that there is chaos in the forest? It helps us be mindful of the fact that we don't have all the answers. We don't know if the goshawk will want to nest in a Douglas-fir tree, a madrone, or a redwood. We don't know which trees will be hit most heavily by an invading insect or disease.

So when we do management in the woods, it's a good idea to make sure that we maintain diversity. That is, we want to maintain trees of different species and age classes so that there is variety over the landscape. This diversity helps create resiliency, which contributes to a healthy forest, functioning well in the midst of and even because of the chaos.

Forest Canopies and Structural Diversity

While on a walk with a friend through an old-growth grove, he commented that in college he had worked as a research assistant for a redwood canopy study. "It's a totally different thing going on up there compared to what you see on the ground," he commented. "There are times when the canopy is so thick that you can't even see the ground."

We know that canopies are important "structures" in the forest. My friend was struck by the canopy's "thickness," or canopy cover. Equally important is the concept of structural diversity. Ideally, the forest should have variation in terms of vertical (from the ground up) and horizontal (moving around from place to place, either on the ground or in the air) structure. This is called vertical and horizontal structural diversity.

What are some examples of components of structural diversity? Gaps are one—they occur when, for example, a tree is blown over in a windstorm. Through the gap, sunlight can reach the forest floor, which might change what plants grow there or how fast they grow. The physical gap as well as the changes in vegetation may in turn change how wildlife uses the space. Other examples include having trees of different ages, different sizes, and different species. Or having snags of varying size classes and stages of decay. Each of these forest "structures" provides its own niche for wildlife.

We understand many of these niches, but it is difficult for us to predict just where they will appear or how they will be used. This underscores the importance of maintaining good diversity within a forest. My friend, for example, described seeing plants growing on tree branches where enough "soil" had formed over the years for the plants to take root. Who (wildlife biologists and botanists aside) would have predicted that?

Looking up into the canopy of second-growth redwoods in Brooktrails Township of Mendocino County.

Stress and Forest Health

Most of us have had our share of stress in our lives, and collectively we understand that getting "stressed out" is harmful to our health. Excessive stress can lead to irritability, susceptibility to colds, and even major illness. But the idea of being "stressed out" is not unique to humans. It is as relevant to trees as it is to people.

What happens when a forest, or more accurately the trees that comprise the forest, get stressed out? When your body and immune systems are healthy, you can fight off cold or flu bugs. Likewise, when you are a healthy tree, you are less susceptible to disease and insect attacks.

Let's look at an example. If you are a vigorous tree, you can put out quite a lot of "pitch." This is very useful if bark beetles are trying to bore inside of you. You just put out your pitch, spitting the beetles out or drowning them in the sticky pitch. Because you've effectively discharged the beetles and prevented them from making more holes in your bark, disease-carrying spores have no way to enter through your bark. Not only have you avoided beetle attack, you've avoided a disease as well.

But if you are a low-vigor tree, you can't put out as much pitch. The beetles, sensing you aren't as good at spitting them out as your neighbors, are actually attracted to you. They successfully make holes in your bark into which those disease-carrying spores find their way. Your future isn't bright, unless you relish the idea of becoming a snag (a standing dead tree).

Healthy forests with healthy trees are much better able to fight off insects or disease. One of the goals of a forestland steward, then, is to work towards creating a healthy forest.

Stress Factors for Trees

When trees get stressed, they become more vulnerable to disease and insect attack. But what are some of the things that can cause a tree to become stressed in the first place?

Trees become stressed when they don't have enough of something they need. The most common stress factor is lack of water. This can happen during long periods of drought, but it can also happen when there are a lot of nearby plants competing for water. This can be competition from other trees, but competition from smaller plants can also be significant. Even deep-rooted tree species may have many fine roots relatively close to the soil surface. If those roots have to compete with a dense layer of shrubs or grasses, there will be less water available for the tree.

Trees also need sunlight, though different species have different needs. Trees that are sun-loving and need plenty of sun to grow well (like pines) are those that will suffer the most stress when other plants, cliffs, or buildings block the available sunlight.

Less intuitive than a tree's need for sunlight and water is the need for soil nutrients and trace minerals. If there are insufficient amounts of critical minerals and nutrients in the soil, you might have a tree with unhealthy-looking yellow-green foliage.

Tree density has a lot to do with how much of what a tree needs it is able to get. Imagine sitting down to your dinner table, with a plateful of food for each person. Each person will leave the table well-satisfied. Now double the number of people, but don't increase the amount of food. Each person will have half of what he or she really wants and needs. No one will starve, but everyone will leave the table hungry and just maybe a bit irritable. Double the number of people again…you get the idea. This brings us to one of the basic forms of forest management—thinning. It's a way to reduce the number of trees competing for finite resources. This gives the trees that are left a full plate of "food," allowing them to be healthy and thrive.

Productivity and Thinning

One of the truths in forestry is that a site is as productive as it is. Foresters think of this in terms of something called "site class." You might get a redwood to grow to a diameter of 15 feet and a height of 250 feet on site class I (the best), but you'd never get the same tree to grow to those same dimensions on site class V (the worst). It just won't happen.

Site class has to do with the fertility of the soil. More specifically, it has to do with soil characteristics and properties like depth, permeability, parent material, nutrient availability, etc. It is generally recognized that the impact of site class is greatest on the height of trees. A poor site will grow short trees, while a good site is capable of growing very tall trees.

Another important factor in how large a tree will grow is the density of trees, or how many trees there are per acre. Trees compete with each other for sunlight, water and soil nutrients, and crowded stands produce smaller diameter trees.

A given site will produce a certain amount of wood. The question is how that wood will be distributed. The growth of the site might be concentrated on a few large trees. Or it might be spread out over a few hundred very small-diameter trees per acre. Think of site productivity as representing a certain sum of money, say $100. Whether you have two $50 bills, ten $10 bills, or a hundred $1 bills, the amount is the same. What changes is the distribution.

When a stand is thinned out by fire or forest management, the remaining trees have more resources available to them, and they grow bigger and faster. In other words, they capture the growth potential of the site, effectively trading in some of the $1 bills for $5 or $10 bills.

Think of this the next time you look at a redwood "fairy ring." Look to see if you can find the original stump around which the fairy ring established itself. Then consider that a site will produce as much wood as it will produce -- the growth that is now spread out among perhaps a dozen trees making up the fairy ring went into that single very large stem long ago.

An old redwood stump is partially surrounded by a "fairy ring" of stump sprouts. Compare the diameter of the stump to the combined diameters of the second-growth trees surrounding it.

The Dynamic Forest and Restoration

Forests are and always have been dynamic systems. In a human lifespan that is very short compared to the life of a forest ecosystem, it's easy to forget that. Natural events such as landslides, high-intensity fires, low-intensity fires, windstorms, and snowstorms have been shaping our forests for thousands of years.

Then humans began to change the face of the forest through many different activities. Native Americans managed the forests for production of food and other necessities. More recently, we expanded human uses that now include activities such as timber harvesting, conversion of forests to agriculture (such as vineyards), conversion to home sites and other development, and recreation that relies heavily on use of roads.

Lately a lot of people have been talking about "restoration," which has become a popular buzzword. But we should ask thequestion, what is it that should be restored? Is the goal a pre-European landscape? Or a landscape that was not managed by even Native Americans? Or is the goal to create a forest that people find aesthetically pleasing, regardless of whether or not that is a true restoration of the vegetation that used to be? The first step in restoration work needs to be a clear understanding of what our goal is.

This forester is hiking through a high-elevation true fir forest to get to a unit in a wilderness area. He is collecting data on unmanaged stands in the Six Rivers National Forest.

A second question is, how do we manage for restoration in a landscape in which humans are an active part? The corollary questions are many. How do we reintroduce fire into a landscape that has been building up fuels for many decades? What is the role of active forest management in restoring forests? What are the impacts on wildlife of the openings and edges created by roads and homes, or of people's dogs, cats and septic systems? How do recreational activities like riding ATVs, mountain bikes or horses impact restoration? How can we reduce or compensate for human impacts? We still have more questions than answers.

Trees and Genetic Diversity

At a meeting held at the Institute of Forest Genetics (IFG) outside of Placerville, the director of the institute gave a fascinating presentation in which he addressed the topic of genetic diversity. I am no expert on genetics but certainly found some of his comments and insights extremely interesting.

If you are a forest landowner, you know that when buying seedlings, you buy from a particular seed zone. (Work on identifying seed zones and their importance was pioneered at the IFG.) You may not realize just how important that is, though. Getting seedlings from the correct seed zone can give you a tree that can have twice the volume as a tree of the same species from another seed zone, according to the IFG director. Both elevation and location are critical, and IFG recommends that your seedlings come from seeds harvested within 500 *feet* of where you will be planting. While that's not realistic for most of us, the point is well taken that seed zones are extremely important.

Another fascinating point was that trees have 10 to 100 times the genetic diversity of humans. This is in part because the cells in a tree divide many more times than the cells in a human before sexual reproduction takes place. There may also be a higher mutation rate in trees than in humans.

But the most interesting point was this – just because the genetic diversity exists doesn't mean that diversity fulfills a useful function. We need to ask the question, how much genetic diversity is really necessary? Some of the diversity may simply be random mutations that don't really help the species adapt at all. Bear in mind that this thought came from a man, the director of IFG, who was emphatic about conserving genetic diversity. He commented that soil regenerates overnight (in "only" a few centuries) compared to how longs it takes to recover genetic diversity once it has been lost.

Visit the website of the Institute of Forest Genetics at http://www.psw.fs.fed.us/ifg.

Learning About Fire – It's Not *If*, It's *When*

Coexisting with Fire

In August of 2002, there were over half a million acres, or some 800 square miles, burning in California and Oregon, according to the National Fire News. Yet as bad as the 2002 fires were, they didn't come as a surprise to those who have seen the immense fuel loadings of recent years.

Those active in forest management and fire suppression have long known the phrase, "It's not *if*, it's *when*," meaning that it's only a matter of time before a fire burns through an area. While we can work to reduce fires caused by humans, we can't do much about lightening strikes that start fires. We always have had fires in the west and we always will.

So our strategy needs to be one of coexisting with fire. How can we do that? Besides simply getting used to the idea that fires *will* come, the single most important thing we can do is to modify fuels on both public and private forest land.

Fuels modification means changing the amount and structure of forest fuels – trees, shrubs, snags, logs and small woody debris. The goal is to have less fuel available to burn, while breaking up the vertical and horizontal continuity of fuels.

Burned area near Rattlesnake Summit, Mendocino County.

Thinning trees, pruning lower branches (live and dead), clearing brush, and removing half-fallen snags are all good ways to break up vertical continuity of fuels. This makes it more difficult for the fire to climb into the canopy. Breaking up horizontal continuity can be done by putting in place shaded fuel breaks (thinned forest stands) or fire lines (cleared to bare soil). This helps stop or slow a fire.

We've all heard about how expensive it is to fight wildfires. It makes much more sense to do what we can in terms of fuels management before the fires come. An ounce of prevention really is worth a pound of cure.

A $147 Million Pound of Cure

The Biscuit Fire that burned in southern Oregon and northern California in the summer of 2002 generated smoke that blew all the way to Mendocino County and beyond. The fires consumed just under half a million acres and cost taxpayers a whopping $147 million, according to the website www.biscuitfire.com. That works out to nearly $300 per acre in fire suppression costs.

So how does that compare to the cost of fuels reduction projects? At a meeting on fuels management in the Sierras in 2001, participants visited fuels reduction project sites and saw a range of fuels reduction methods. Some sites were simply burned (control burns to reduce vegetation), others were thinned before burning, and still others had vegetation removed with no burning. Costs for these fuel reduction projects varied widely, from a low of about $100 per acre to a high of around $450 per acre.

When you look at the cost of such projects from the perspective of an individual landowner with 40 acres, for example, $4,000 - $18,000 for fuels reduction sounds prohibitively expensive. But when you think of it in terms of the cost to the taxpayer, fire suppression on that 40 acres would have cost us about $12,000, using the cost per acre of fighting the Biscuit Fire as a baseline. That's in the same ballpark.

Now consider that in planning fuels reduction projects, it makes sense to place fuel breaks in logical areas, for example along ridges and existing roads. In other words, you can do a lot to protect a hillside by strategically locating the areas where you do fuels reduction. You might need to manage vegetation on 10-25% of the land area in order to dramatically improve the ability of firefighters to stop a fire.

Let's assume that the area on which vegetation management would have been needed to reduce the Biscuit Fire's intensity and make firefighting efforts more effective would have been a full 25%. If the same amount of money had been spent on prevention as was spent on the $147 million pound of cure, nearly $1,200 could have been spent per acre. The actual cost of projects in the Sierras indicates that projects can be done for much less than that. That makes fuel reduction projects look much more sensible in terms of cost. Either way, it's we the taxpayers who are footing the bill.

Ground, Ladder and Crown Fuels

We all know that fuels feed fires, but what's less intuitive is that different types of fuels feed fires in different ways. There are three kinds of fuels – ground, ladder, and crown. Ground fuels are those on the ground, like herbaceous vegetation, downed logs, and leaf litter. Crown fuels include the tops of trees, or the canopy. And ladder fuels include anything that helps a fire climb from the ground to the crown fuels. Common ladder fuels include tall grasses, shrubs, and tree branches, both live and dead.

Reducing ground fuels breaks up the horizontal continuity, reducing how quickly the fire can spread and limiting the amount of material available to burn. Similarly, reducing ladder fuels breaks up the vertical continuity, limiting how quickly a fire can climb upwards. In both cases, the end result is a fire that is less intense and less likely to climb into the tree canopy.

While researchers tell us that it is most important to reduce surface and ladder fuels, it's also helpful to reduce crown fuels. Spacing trees out so that there is room between the individual tree crowns does two things. First, it makes it more difficult for the fire to spread from treetop to treetop. Second, creating spaces allows for the heat from a ground fire to escape upwards, rather than being trapped by tree branches.

Management of vegetation for fuels, by reducing and breaking up horizontal and vertical continuity of fuels, results in fires spreading more slowly and having a more difficult time reaching the canopy. In some cases, fires in the tree canopy have even dropped to the ground in areas that have been properly treated for fuels reduction. The key is to be proactive and to do the vegetation management *before* the fire comes.

Fire Cycles

It's not at all uncommon to hear the phrase that fire is "a natural part of the landscape." But what does that really mean? There is a whole science devoted to "fire ecology," looking at how fire helps shape the landscape and interacts with the biological resources in that landscape. But let's look at one particularly important concept in fire ecology, the "fire cycle."

Where there is fire, there is a fire cycle. The fire cycle is the number of years, on average, that a fire historically moved through the area. It is also called the "fire return interval."

All our forest ecosystems in California have fire cycles. Even the coastal areas have fire cycles, though they are very long, measured in hundreds of years. But in very hot, dry areas, fire cycles might be as short as every 1-7 years. In inland areas of California's coastal counties, fires might have come through on average every 15-40 years before the days of fire suppression. The number of years depends on many variables such as the forest or vegetation type and the size of the area you are considering.

When the fire cycle is allowed to function, the result is frequent, low-intensity fires. But when the fire cycle is interrupted, the stage is set for a catastrophic fire.

Think of a few oaks tree loosing their leaves every year. If you burned one year's accumulation of fallen twigs and leaves, you'd have a well behaved little fire with flame lengths of a few inches to a couple of feet or so. The base of the oak trees would get a little warm and might even blacken a bit.

But allow the fallen twigs and leaves to accumulate for 50 years before you decide to burn. Some will have decomposed, but you'll have a lot of fuel for that fire. Instead of a small "cool" fire, you'll have a raging inferno whose flames will most likely reach into the tree itself, burning leaves and killing trees.

Prescribed burning is a way forest managers now use to reintroduce fire into the forest. The idea is to mimic the fire cycles we have disrupted.

"Hot" vs. "Cool" Fires – What's the Difference?

Before the days of fire suppression, wildfires tended to be of lower intensity than those we are experiencing today. That's of course because fires occurred regularly, burned freely, and had available as fuel only what had accumulated since the last fire. While there were certainly some large catastrophic fires, on the whole available fuels were less abundant than they are today, and so the intensity of the fires was lower.

A low-intensity, "cool" fire is still hot, but there are important ways in which it is different from a high-intensity, "hot" fire. A low-intensity fire burns at lower temperatures and remains in a single location for a shorter period of time. For these reasons, a "cool" fire's impact on vegetation, soil, and soil micro-organisms is fundamentally different from the impact of a "hot" fire.

Think of the "fire-walkers," those people who walk on coals. They brave several barefoot steps across hot coals and, for the most part, emerge on the other side in good shape. The amount of time each foot is in contact with the coals is brief, and they are walking across coals, not through tall flames. Common sense tells us that they would be crazy to try to spend an hour standing on a coal without moving, or to walk through a bonfire, as the result would be very different.

It's the same principle with forest fires and their effects. We know, for example, that soil temperatures rise during a fire. The more intense the fire (in terms of duration or temperature), the higher the soil temperature will get and the deeper that rise in soil temperature will go. If temperatures get hot enough, there can be chemical and physical changes in the soil, the effects of which last long after the fire is gone. One such change is that after an intense or repeated fire, soil porosity can decrease, meaning it will be less able to hold water.

Looking at the vegetation, we know that the bark of trees protects them against fire. But the bark that can provide effective shielding from a cool fire will itself heat up if the fire is intense enough. This allows the cambium layer (the living part of the tree's trunk) underneath the bark to rise in temperature, injuring or even killing the tree.

There are many other examples of cool fires being more "forest-friendly" than hot fires. As we reintroduce fire, it's important to recognize that high-intensity wildfires are fundamentally different from and more destructive than the smaller, "cool" fires that can help keep our forest ecosystems in balance.

Tree Bark and Fire

In California's forests, there will be fires. These fires can be beneficial, for example by thinning out a stand of trees. But why does a fire kill one tree and leave another standing?

Tree boles are one of three areas in which the tree is vulnerable to fire. The other two areas are foliage and roots. If the fire is hot enough, it can kill the living tissue in any of these three zones of the tree.

Bark protects tree boles from fire. The bark's thickness is the most important predictor of whether or not the tree's living tissue under the bole will survive. Scientists have developed a formula that shows a direct correlation between bark thickness and survival. According to the formula, if you have a 500-degree Celsius fire come through, the trees with bark that is 1/10 of an inch thick will survive less than two minutes. But bigger trees with 1-inch thick bark will survive almost 20 minutes. The thicker the bark, the longer the tree can withstand the heat of the fire.

Besides the thickness, the type of bark makes a difference. A flat, "platey" bark will tend to have higher temperatures in a fire than bark with "fissures," or what look like cracks. Another factor is the time of year, as moisture content in bark is lower in summer months.

Finally, bark of different tree species vary in flammability. The actual structure and density of the bark of different tree species offer varying levels of protection from fire.

The thick bark of the Ponderosa pine helps protect the tree's living cambium layer from wildfires.

When you walk through the forest, it's interesting to think about which trees would survive fires of various intensities. And look for clues…fire scars on tree boles are a clear indication that those trees not only can but have survived a fire.

Roots, Foliage and Fire

We've looked at how the bole of a tree is protected from fire by bark. But there are two other parts of a tree that can be damaged by fire: the roots and the foliage.

It might be surprising to find out that bark plays a role in protecting a tree's roots from fire damage. That's because the tree's roots are surrounded by thin bark. Fine roots, which have very thin bark, and roots that are found closer to the ground surface are more likely to suffer damage than thicker roots that are better protected by bark and/or soil. So the roots of trees with shallow rooting habits (Sitka spruce or grand fir) are much more likely to be damaged or killed by a fire's damage to the roots than trees with deeper rooting habits (Douglas-fir or ponderosa pine).

Damage to foliage is determined by the tree's branching habits and foliage flammability, as well as other factors like how hot the fire is, air temperature, and wind speed. Foliage flammability is fairly straightforward and intuitive. It is related to the content of resins or oils in the leaves or needles as well as their moisture content.

The effect of branching habits on foliage damage is a little more complex. Trees that have low and dense branches (grand fir or hemlock) are more likely to have their foliage damaged than trees that have branching habits that are higher (Douglas fir) or less dense (ponderosa pine). This is true even if the fire itself does not reach into the crown of the tree, because the hot gases above the fire can kill the foliage and buds. And the higher percentage of a tree's live crown that is killed by a fire, the lower the likelihood the tree will survive.

Fire and Redwoods

At first, you might think that fire doesn't have much of a place in redwood ecology. After all, redwoods tend to grow in moist areas-coastal areas, drainages and alluvial flats. But if you've ever seen a "goosepen" or a fire scar on a redwood, it's clear that fire helped shape the redwood forests.

While redwood is not a fire-dependent species, fire does favor it. Historically, low- and small-intensity fires (average flame lengths of under about 1.5 meters) would go through these forests, sometimes burning for weeks or even months. Overstory redwoods with thick bark often were not seriously damaged. Even redwoods whose crowns were scorched could resprout new crowns, as long as the fire wasn't too hot. But Douglas-fir, grand fir and hemlock whose crowns were seriously scorched would die, thus favoring the redwood. One very interesting study in a coastal redwood stand showed that there were redwoods of all different ages. But the Douglas-fir tended to be in a few different age groups, presumably each age group having been established after a fire event. And the grand fir and hemlock (less fire-resistant than Douglas-fir) were all young, having come in since the last fire.

How often did fire historically go through redwood forests? In moist sites along the coast, some have estimated the fire-return interval (how many years on average between fires) at as long as 500-600 years. But in inland areas, the interval was much shorter, often less than every 50 years. Data shows that at Humboldt Redwoods State Park, the fire-return interval was about 31 years. For the area near Muir Woods, the historic return interval was about 25 years.

Next time you take a walk through a redwood forest, look around for the black marks on the trees that help tell the story of when fire went through the forest.

Salvage Harvest after Fires

Most people are familiar with the concept of salvage harvesting after natural disasters such as wildfires and windstorms. What is less well understood is why it is important, if salvage logging is to be done, to do so in a timely way.

Events like fires or windstorms wound trees. One effect is to leave the tree weakened. Just as you are more likely to catch a cold when you are run down, a tree is less able to tolerate stress when it is in a weakened condition. Damaged trees are vulnerable to stressors like drought or insects that a healthy, vigorous tree can withstand. Another effect is to provide a point of entry for damaging agents. Just as a cut in your hand is an entry point for bacteria that cause infection, damaged bark or a blown-out top provide easy entry into a tree by fungus, bacteria and insects.

When a tree has been killed by fire or another event, it will begin to rot. Different species rot at varying rates and are susceptible to different kinds of rot. White fir, for example, rots very quickly. Within a year, 20% of the volume of wood may be rotted. Within two years, the figure will be closer to 50%. Other species such as Douglas-fir take a couple of years for significant rot to take hold, first in the sapwood and next in the heartwood. Pines tend to rot more slowly than white fir but more quickly than Douglas-fir. Pine is also impacted by something called "bluestain," which is a fungus that causes the wood color to change, resulting in loss of commercial value.

Whether you do salvage logging or not is a personal decision. And the goal of salvage logging should not be to remove every dead and damaged tree. Both dead trees (called snags) and fallen dead trees (called large woody debris) are important for wildlife habitat. But you can have too much of a good thing. The snags and downed woody debris you leave after a fire or windstorm will become fuel for the next fire that occurs.

For a copy of portions of the Forest Practice Rules pertaining to salvage logging, call the Forest Stewardship Helpline at 800-738-8733.

Smoke & Fire

In northern California, our wildfires might be caused by any of a number of ignition sources: summer lightening strikes, escaped campfires, stray sparks, or even arson. Whatever the source, where there is fire, there is smoke.

The amount of smoke generated and where that smoke ends up depend on a number of conditions. Foresters involved in prescribed burning or burning of slash piles consider factors such as fuel moisture content, air temperature, wind speed and direction, in addition to the type of fuel burning and how it is likely to burn. A flaming fire, for example, produces less smoke than and only about half of the particulate matter of a smoldering fire.

The smoke from forest fires may influence forest health. There is speculation that the smoke helps keep certain insect populations down. Looking at it the other way, fire suppression, and therefore smoke prevention, may allow those same insect populations to increase. (You might look for your own anecdotal evidence of this principal by noticing whether or not there are many bugs in the car or truck of a friend who smokes heavily.)

Because we live in an area where there is little summer rainfall and summer lightening strikes can occur, it is very likely that our typical air quality in the summer is much better now than it was before fire suppression. When we suppress our wildfires, we also suppress smoke emissions. Though we might find the smoke from wildfires and forest management activities annoying at times, it is important to remember that smoke is a naturally occurring part of our fire-dependent ecosystems.

When Smoke Gets in Your Eyes

Have you wondered what is in that smoke that you see, smell and breathe during a severe fire?

Generally, carbon dioxide and water vapor account for about 90% of the smoke. The other 10% is a combination of particulate matter, carbon monoxide, hydrocarbons, and VOCs (volatile organic compounds).

When you see smoke, you are looking at particulate matter, which is basically soot or ash from the fire. Much of the particulate matter generated by wildfires is small enough (under 2.5 micrometers) to be a potential problem for human health when the particles get into your lungs. If you use an air filtration system in your home, that will help reduce the level of particulate matter in the air you breathe.

How much particulate matter is produced depends on the type of fuel and how it burns. A smoldering fire, for example, will produce more (as much as two or three times more) particulates than a flaming fire.

Particulate matter also acts as a nucleus for hydrocarbons. One type of hydrocarbon, aldehydes, contributes to the sting and irritation when smoke gets in your eyes.

People closest to the fire lines, where the smoke is the most dense, have the highest health risk. This is particularly true for carbon monoxide, a gas produced primarily when a fire is smoldering or has just been put out.

Smoke can travel many miles. During the Biscuit Fire of 2002 in Oregon and areas just over the border with California, many areas of northern California, including Mendocino County, were blanketed by smoke for several days. Smoke doesn't have any respect for ownership boundaries or political borders.

The Biology of Soil

When we think of forest soil, most of us think of the impacts of soil erosion on our watercourses and fish populations. But our soil is a precious and living resource itself.

Of course we know that soil provides physical structure in which plants grow. The type and structure of the soil, the size and number of micropores and macropores, also influence how much water and how many nutrients are available to plants. In short, the type and condition of the soil has a lot to do with the fertility of a site. But beyond this, there is a biology of the soil.

First, the soil is home to many critters such as worms, mullosks, millipedes, springtails, and, yes, termites. These critters help in the decomposition of everything from leaf litter to downed logs. They also help churn the soil, which improves aeration and soil structure. These critters as well as some vertebrates do on a small scale what you do as you turn manure into your garden to improve the soil.

Second, soil contains "microflora." These include bacteria, fungi, algae, and a group called actinomycetes, which are a lot like fungi. Of this group, the fungi are of special importance, as they include mycorrhiza. You might think of these of "magic mycorrhiza," as they provide many benefits to plants – they help in nutrient uptake, can help increase the longevity and branchiness of roots, and can even help in inhibiting attack from other fungi.

There's a rich and diverse world in the dirt beneath your feet that is a vital and thriving part of the forest.

Soil and seedlings in a second-growth redwood forest.

Productive Soil – Like Money in the Bank

Good forest soil is like money in the bank. Each year it generates "interest" in the form of the trees, shrubs, herbs and wildlife that it supports. If managed carefully and properly, it can provide a perpetual stream of benefits.

An important point to remember is that all soils are not alike. Some are inherently more productive than others. How productive they are depends in large part on depth, texture, and the amount of organic matter available.

The depth of a soil is basically how far you can dig until you reach bedrock. A soil has different layers, called horizons. The top layers are a good source of nutrients. The lower layers store some nutrients but most importantly hold water that plants can take up during dry periods. The overall depth and structure effect a plant's growth and rooting depth.

The texture of a soil also affects its productivity. A soil with too tight a texture (with a lot of clay) makes plant growth difficult because it holds water and nutrients very tightly, making it hard for plants to absorb them. Very loose soils (with a lot of sand) lose water and nutrients too rapidly. The most productive soils have a medium texture with a good mixture of particles of sand, clay, and silt. They hold water and nutrients tightly enough so that they don't flush out of the soil but loosely enough so that plants can absorb them.

Organic matter comes from plants or animals. Mostly located near the ground surface, organic matter is extremely important because it helps the soil hold more water and is a great source of nutrients. The available nutrients and even the acidity (pH) of a soil are influenced by the amount and type of soil organic matter. Generally, the darker the soil, the more organic matter it has.

For people living or working in the woods, it's important to remember that it is difficult to make poor forest soils more productive, but bad management practices can cause good soils to lose their productivity through processes like compaction or soil erosion. Protecting your forest soil is like protecting your money in the bank.

Soil – Like a Sponge

After a heavy winter rain, you can see the water level in creeks and rivers rise, sometimes dramatically. What you don't see is the very large amount of water that is stored in the ground. The ground acts like a giant sponge, absorbing water that will be available after the winter rains.

There are two important kinds of water storage below the ground surface -- ground water and soil moisture.

Ground water is basically saturated soil, like an underground swamp. There is an area of permanent saturation, and above that an area that is sometimes saturated, sometimes not. The upper surface of the saturated area, or groundwater, is called the water table. In this zone under the water table, there is rock and soil, but there's no air to support plant root growth.

Above the water table is a zone where plant roots can thrive. In this zone, soil contains both air and water.

How well a soil can absorb new rainfall has to do with factors like how much water it can potentially hold, how much water it is already holding, and how deep it is. Soils vary in the amount of moisture they can hold because they vary greatly in texture, porosity, depth, etc If you think of soil moisture storage as like a sponge holding water, it becomes clear that it can only hold so much. How much it can hold depends on the type and size of the sponge, and how wet it already is.
The ability of soil to store water is one reason to minimize soil compaction. By reducing the size of soil pores, we reduce its ability to store water. And that means more winter runoff and less water that can be squeezed out of "the sponge" in those dry months.

Saturated Soils and Creep

With heavy winter or spring rains, the "flooded" signs sometimes are put out on county roads. That's a very clear sign that, just like a sponge reaches a point where it can't absorb more water, so too do soils become saturated.

Soils that are saturated today may be able to absorb more water tomorrow. That's because water "percolates" down, making it possible for the soil to absorb more water. Soils vary considerably in their percolation rates. That's why "perc tests" need to be done before installing a leach field for a septic system.

The saturation of soils is a factor in soil movement. As you drive along the highways in some areas, you can see examples of one kind of soil movement commonly called soil "creep." What you see from the road is the soil is moving slowly downward and onto the road. This is particularly noticeable in relatively steep grasslands where there are few or no large roots to help keep the soil in place.

Why does soil creep? Think of what it's like to walk on heavy clay soil that is saturated with water. It's very slippery. When soils become saturated, the friction between the particles of soil is reduced. The particles can slip and slide if the slope is steep enough and the pull of gravity strong enough. Sometimes the movement is very slight, measured in inches or even fractions of an inch per year.

Another factor contributing to soil creep is the expansion and contraction of soil particles. That's why a hillslope might begin to shift as things dry out after winter rains.

It's always best to avoid driving on saturated soils. Besides the obvious advantage of not getting stuck, not driving on roads when they are wet (unless they are well rocked) helps keep our streams clear by preventing the movement of soil into watercourses.

Soil Erosion

A certain amount of erosion is natural and in fact is fact healthy for the ecosystem. Gravels continually move downstream in watercourses, and it is through erosion that new gravels are put back into the upper reaches of those streams. Too much erosion, however, can cause problems, reducing soil fertility and water quality.

What causes erosion to be severe in some areas and minor elsewhere? It is a combination of many factors, including the amount and intensity of precipitation, the texture of the soil, the steepness of the slope, and ground cover (from vegetation, rocks, etc.).

The first three factors don't change much. In general, given the same kind of vegetative cover, you expect areas with high-intensity precipitation, sandy or silty soils, and steep slopes to be the most erosive. Soils with a lot of clay that receive less intense precipitation and are on gentle slopes tend to erode less.

The factor that is most subject to change is the amount and type of ground cover. When fires burn an area or when vegetation is removed as part of timber operations, building a house or a road, the susceptibility of the soil to erosion is increased.

Roads are especially likely to cause increased rates of erosion because, in addition to removing ground cover, they can significantly change drainage patterns. A road that has a lot of rock and one that is "hydrologically invisible" (that gets the water off the road as quickly as possible, mimicking natural drainage patterns) has the best chance of not causing increased erosion.

I've seen one property on which soil that eroded from roads and collected in a pond was dredged up and put back on to the roads. The roads were then rebuilt to prevent future erosion problems. It was a good solution, but very time-consuming and costly. It's a lot simpler and less expensive to manage from the beginning to prevent erosion, keeping the soil where it belongs.

"Fun Guy" in the Forest

Do you ever wonder how to pronounce "fungi"? Just remember what the fern said to the mushroom: "You're such a fun guy!"

"Fungi" is of course the plural of "fungus" (some people say "funguses," which is also correct). There are many kinds of fungi, including molds and mildews, mushrooms, rusts, etc. Some common characteristics of fungi are that they don't have chlorophyll, help decompose other material, and reproduce by means of spores.

In the forest, fungi are important for two reasons. One, they are decomposers. In many forest soils, they are the majority of the decomposers, breaking down limbs, logs, leaves, and other dead material. Some fungi form what look like long, thin strings, called hyphae. These are often white or yellowish and, particularly in the upper layers of soil, can be very abundant.

One study in Scotland years ago measured over 18 feet of hyphae (5.6 meters) per cubic centimeter of soil! The density of hyphae in our soils isn't so high, but next time you are in the woods, run your hands through the soil. If you feel or see little whitish or yellowish strands that snap, those are the hyphae of soil fungi. Some fungi have hyphae that are dark-colored, but these can be confused with fine plant roots.

The other important function of fungi is in helping plants take up nutrients. Certain kinds of fungi form a special relationship with tree roots that helps both the fungi and the tree. It is a symbiotic (win-win) relationship in which the fungi decompose material in or near the tree roots, and for reasons not entirely understood, the presence of fungi allows the tree roots to take up nutrients more efficiently.

Scientists have found that seedling survival, height and weight are all much higher in seedlings that are planted in soils with these specialized fungi than those that aren't. The effect of the fungi has been likened to the effect of fertilizing with nitrogen.

Next time you are in the woods, look in the soil and on the logs to see if you can spot a forest "fun guy" or two.

The Riparian World

Anadromous Fish

A lot of time and money has been and continues to be spent by public agencies and private landowners on north coast to protect and improve fish habitat. The focus is usually on anadromous fish, more familiar to most people as salmon, steelhead, as well as shad.

The word "anadromous" literally means "running upward." This refers to the fact that these fish go up rivers to spawn. Anadromous fish are born and reared in fresh water, then migrate to the ocean to grow and mature. They eventually return to fresh water to reproduce, usually swimming up their native streams.

The health of anadromous fish populations is often taken as a barometer of the quality of forestry practices. Over the years a myriad of forest practice rules has been passed to help protect fish habitat by requiring certain standards in on-the-ground work. There are rules regarding the retention of shade cover over streams critical to maintaining the low stream temperatures needed by the fish. Other rules are in place to ensure a current and future supply of large woody debris that will help create and maintain pools or other stream functions and characteristics used and needed by the fish. Still other rules aim to reduce sediment movement into the watercourses the fish use for spawning.

What is less often talked about is the host of other issues that impact the health of the anadromous fish populations. Populations are reduced by sea mammals that feed upon the fish, particularly at the mouths of rivers. Road culverts and dams, unless properly designed for fish passage, become barriers to migrating fish. And any road, whether used as a personal driveway, a recreational trail, an agricultural access road, or a forestry road, can result in small or large amounts of sediment deposited in the streams.

It is important when we think of fish health to remember that there are many factors and many players involved. All need to be equally addressed if we are to ensure the health of our anadromous fisheries.

In this riparian area, note the overhanging branches of the hardwoods, as well as the large pool that can be used by fish.

Riparian Vegetation

When visiting a friend in Scotland who lives by a creek that supports an Atlantic salmon population, we went down to look at the banks of the creek. There was a lot of active bank erosion happening, so we took a close look to see what might be done to stabilize the banks and slow the erosion.

Not surprisingly, the areas that were the most

stable were those that had riparian vegetation. Along this particular creek, the vegetation consists almost exclusively of bushy willows. Establishing more riparian vegetation -- planting more willows

-- would help stabilize the banks of the creek (which the Scots call the "water").

Often when we think of riparian vegetation we think of large trees. While trees are certainly necessary to provide inputs of large woody debris, other types of vegetation are equally important in terms of improving bankslope stability, providing nutrient inputs, and keeping water temperatures low.

In areas prone to erosion, soil that would otherwise be eroded by flowing water can be held in place by the roots of riparian vegetation. Both large and fine roots add to the soil stability. Some plants provide a better root system and therefore more stability. The non-native arundo is an example of a plant that grows well in riparian areas but provides very little soil stability.

Riparian vegetation is also important in the food chain. Decaying leaves that have fallen from trees and shrubs that overhang the bank can be an important food source for insects. Many of these insects will be eaten by fish, birds or other creatures. Insects also fall from overhanging vegetation directly into the water, often becoming food for fish.

Finally, overhanging vegetation provides shade cover that helps keep stream temperatures low. In areas where summers are hot and dry, the presence of shade can mean the difference between lethal and non-lethal stream temperatures for fish.

One of the most interesting aspects of working with natural resources is seeing how general principles apply no matter where you are. Regardless of political boundaries or what continent you are on, riparian vegetation is vital to healthy streams and fish populations.

Streamside Shade Cover

One of the critical issues related to fisheries and forestry is how much shade to leave over watercourses. What everyone understands is that fish need low water temperatures and that shade cover in the summer can play a critical role in keeping stream temperatures down. (It's an interesting experiment to take a thermometer down to a stream and compare a temperature taken in water that is shaded with a temperature taken in water that is receiving direct sunlight.)

The debate is not over whether or not shade canopy is important. It is. The debate is over how much shade canopy is needed, where it is needed, and on what kind of streams it is needed. To take an obvious example, let's suppose there is a stream that doesn't have water flowing in it from April until November. The amount of shade cover over the watercourse isn't going to have any impact on water temperature during the summer months when stream temperature is an issue, because there isn't any water there.

A less clear example relates to where shade canopy should be left. Under current forestry rules, shade canopy has to be left over the entire watercourse protection zone, which extends from 50 to 150 feet, depending on how steep the slopes are how big the watercourse is, on either side of the watercourse. The same rules are applied throughout that entire protection zone.

Now shift gears for a moment and think about your garden. If you want to increase the amount of sunlight to the garden, where would you cut trees? Would you cut trees 50 or 100 or 150 feet from the garden? Probably not. You'd cut the trees right next to it. Conversely, if you want to increase shade to watercourses, it makes sense to concentrate on leaving trees closest to the stream channels.

As so often is the case when we manage natural resources, a one-size-fits-all approach often doesn't allow for using common sense to make wise management decisions.

Riparian Areas and the Harvest Plan

Protection of the beneficial uses of water and riparian areas is one of the most important, time-consuming, and costly aspects of preparing a timber harvest plan in California. In his or her plan area, the forester has the daunting task of adequately protecting all water supplies, which must be located, classified, mapped and flagged. Seeps, springs, seasonal and streams all must be evaluated by an RPF who classifies them as I (capable of supporting fish), II (capable of supporting aquatic life), or III (capable of transporting sediment to a class I or II).

Depending on the size of the plan, this in itself can take weeks, as the forester typically walks the length of every watercourse on the plan area a minimum of once, and often two or more times. All water sources and watercourses must be readily identifiable and adequately protected in the field. Often this means flagging buffer zones of 50 to 150 feet on both sides of a creek or spring and marking with paint any trees that will be removed from the buffer zone. Many class III watercourses run only a handful of times per year, and some are so shallow and covered by debris that, to an untrained eye, they do not look like a watercourse at all.

The Forest Practice Rules have numerous restrictions regarding overstory and understory canopy retention, recruitment of large woody debris, watercourse crossings, and heavy equipment operations in riparian areas, just to name a few. In the plan write-up as well as in the field, a tremendous amount of attention is given to the specifics of operations in and near water and riparian areas. Watercourse crossing specifications, exceptions to the standards rules, etc. are described in what can only be called excruciating detail.

One section of the write-up is devoted to cumulative effects of the proposed harvest in the local watershed. This analysis considers the impacts of previous and future harvests, in addition to giving a detailed consideration of a wide range of issue addressing the watershed, watercourses, and water quality, as well as soil productivity, wildlife habitat, and timber resources. Exactly how detailed the cumulative impacts section should be and who should pay for collecting the endless data needed as well as the watershed analysis itself is a hotly contested issue.

Tree Species

The Douglas-fir

One of the most common tree species in our coniferous forests from the coast to the Sierras is the Douglas-fir. Named after the botanist David Douglas, its scientific name is *Pseudotsuga*, meaning "false hemlock." Douglas-fir grows up to 250 feet tall and 4-6 feet in diameter on good sites. It seeds in very well on disturbed soil and is often found in pure stands, or as part of a species mix. Old trees have very tall, clear boles, and Douglas-fir wood is valued for its strength, light weight, and decay resistance. It is used extensively for structural lumber, like 2x4s, 2x6s, and plywood. Douglas-fir seeds are used as food by squirrels, mice, birds, and other wildlife.

Douglas-fir has soft, green needles about one inch long that grow all around the twig, giving the branchlets a "bottle-brush" appearance. In the spring, this new growth is a beautiful shade of light green adorning the branch tips. The cones are brown, three to four inches long, and they often litter the forest floor beneath the tree.

The cones are easily recognized if you know their story. It's said that long ago, Owl was pursuing Mouse. Mouse looked in vain for a place to hide to save her life, and at last she spied the Douglas-fir cone. She wriggled her way up into the cone as far as she could but was too large to fit entirely inside the cone. Her backside, including her hind legs and tail, remained exposed. This confused Owl, however, and Mouse lived to teach this trick to the other mice. To this day, you can see their hind legs and tails sticking out of every Douglas-fir cone. Foresters call these "exposed bracts." See if you can find the "mice" in the Douglas-fir cones!

Can you find the "mice" hiding in this Douglas-fir cone?

Black Oak

Each year as autumn approaches, we look forward to the annual display of colors provided by our local deciduous trees. The leaves of the California black oak, *Quercus kelloggii,* contribute some beautiful yellows to that display.

Black oaks are found over much of California, up to about 8,000 feet in elevation. The Forest Service reports that in our state, black oaks cover more area than any other hardwood species. You can find them associated with conifers such as Douglas-fir, pine, or redwood, or with other hardwoods. This is in contrast with white oak, which you would expect to find more in meadows.

Black oak gets its name from its bark, which is dark when compared to white oak bark. An easier way to identify this tree, though, is to look at its leaves. The 4-8" leaves will have thin bristles on the tip of the lobes of the leaves. And the leaf itself will be a glossy dark green.

Black oak acorns were used as a food source by Native Americans in many different parts of what is now California. Harvested in the fall, the acorns were leached to remove the tannins before being ground and made into porridge, soup, or bread.

Black oak acorns today provide an important food source for wildlife. Some species, like squirrels, may get half of their diet from black oak acorns. Beyond providing an important food source, black oak trees provide cavities for dens or nesting, shade, and browse for deer.

Generally, black oaks live 100-200 years. Some will live longer, as long as 500 years in exceptional cases.

At maturity, the tree is typically 1-4 feet in diameter and 50-80 feet in height. Of course individuals may be much bigger than this. The National Champion black oak, recorded in the national Big Trees registry, measures some 28' in circumference (about 9 feet in diameter) and is 124 feet tall. It is located near Grants Pass in Oregon.

The Coast Redwood

California's north coast is of course home to one of three redwood species – the coastal redwood, or S*equoia sempervirens*. This redwood is not to be confused with the Giant sequoia found in the Sierras (and in Europe, where scattered trees have been planted since the 1800s) or the dawn redwood, discovered in China in the 1940s.

The scientific name of the coast redwood, *sempervirens*, means "always-living." Indeed, the tree can live to 2000 years of age or more. Given the right density of trees and soil conditions, the redwood can grow to diameters of up to 21 feet and heights exceeding 300 feet. More commonly, the tree grows 250-275 feet in height and 8-12 feet in diameter where soil conditions are good and stands are not too crowded.

The redwood tree is most unusual among conifers for its ability to stump-sprout. Just like many hardwood trees, a redwood that is harvested or killed by fire will send up sprouts from its still-living (but very shallow) root system. This ring of sprouts around the original stump is what creates the so-called "fairy ring."

The stump-sprouts help account for the tree's resilience to fire and flood. Remarkably, a redwood that is partially buried by dirt deposited from a flood will actually send out new roots, adjusting itself to up to 2 feet or more of new soil. Stump-sprouts also allow for the establishment of new trees following fires, which historically occurred every few hundred years in the coastal redwood zone.

It is ironic that one of the largest trees in the world has some of the smallest seeds. The seeds do best on bare dirt, but the fact is that many of the seeds never germinate. The redwood relies more heavily on stump-sprouts than seed sprouts for successful reproduction.

Our coastal redwoods also produce the heaviest stands of timber in the world. Research has shown that they exceed nearly every other species in producing wood volume in second-growth forests. When a redwood forest is thinned, even large, old trees will respond well and begin to grow more quickly. The key is the interconnectedness of the root system. When one tree is removed, the water and nutrients it received immediately become available to the remaining trees.

Our redwoods are a precious resource. Wise management benefits the redwoods, people and the wildlife that make use of the forest and the resources it offers.

Madrone

One of the most common hardwood trees in our western forests is the beautiful Pacific madrone, also known by the scientific name of *Arbutus menziesii*. Madrone is most easily recognized by its distinctive papery, reddish bark that peels off as the tree grows. Many people think of the excellent firewood that this species provides, but it has many values beyond that.

The madrone is of great benefit to wildlife. You may have seen flocks of birds descend upon a madrone to consume its bright red berries. Mammals also eat the berries, which can be an important food source. The tree also provides nesting spots, and I have even seen goshawks nesting in a small madrone over in the Covelo area.

A few woodworkers use madrone wood for furniture, bowls, and other items. Because of challenges in drying and working with the wood, however, it is not commonly used. But the deep, rich red wood is as gorgeous as it is hard and durable.

Madrone is a species that benefited from periodic fires. Like redwood, madrone sends up new sprouts from its root system after a fire. It does well in a variety of climates, from very dry to very wet. In drought, however, it becomes more susceptible to a canker fungus that causes die-back in the crown of the tree.

Although the tree is common, it is rare to find pure stands of it. The few pure stands I have seen have been breathtakingly beautiful with a light, golden color from above and below. The leaves of the litter layer are brown and yellow, the bark is orange, red and brown, and the leaves, depending on the time of year, range from yellow to green.

This mature madrone tree gives us beauty as well as berries and nesting sites for birds.

The range of this tree is very broad. You can find madrone as far north as British Columbia and as far south as southern California. Wherever you find it, it is a delight.

Sugar Pine

Driving into town one day in early May, I noticed some new cones forming on a sugar pine tree. The sugar pine is a beautiful tree that can grow to 250 feet tall and 10 feet in diameter. It is never found in pure stands except in small, scattered areas. Some foresters describe the bark as jigsaw puzzle-like, and old trees have a characteristic purplish-brown bark of scaly ridges. Its needles, borne in bundles of five, are shorter than those of ponderosa pine, whose needles are borne in bundles of three.

But the sugar pine's most distinguishing characteristic is its crop of incredibly large cones, up to 26 inches long, that hang on the very tips of the branches. It's said that the cones are collected by brave souls who climb the trees and jump up and down on the branches until the cones finally shake loose. Others choose the simpler method of shooting the cones off the tree.

A lumber species, sugar pine is used for moulding, cabinets, and wood-framed windows. Native Americans used the seeds for food and a sugary substance from the bark, called pinitol, for food and eyewash.

Sugar pine is susceptible to bark beetles and an introduced disease called white pine blister rust. CCC crews during the Depression fought this disease, whose alternate host is the gooseberry. The blister rust effects five-needle pine species, of which sugar pine is one (and Western white pine is another.) Work has been done for several years to find genetically "rust-resistant" sugar pine, but the blister rust remains a very real threat to this majestic species.

The Pacific Dogwood

Do you notice the dogwoods each year in the spring? That's the time of year they are hard to miss, with their beautiful white flowers. How can you identify this species when it is not flowering? Foresters know the trick to be able to easily recognize the dogwood. By its "bark."

Seriously, though, there is a trick to identifying the dogwood. Notice the leaves, which have strong veins. Carefully tear a leaf in half, breaking the veins, and slowly separate the halves by half an inch or so. You will see a milky-white sap that stretches between the halves, somewhat like stringy, melted cheese. Other members of the dogwood family, which includes trees, shrubs, and herbs, have this characteristic milky-white sap in the leaves.

The tree's bark is smooth and may have thin scaly plates near the base of the tree. Contrary to the old forester's myth, it is not the easiest way to identify this species.

Pacific dogwood (scientific name *Cornus nuttallii*) occurs naturally as a small tree, seldom larger than 60 feet tall or 20 inches in diameter. It is often much smaller than that, and it sometimes looks more like a bush than a tree. It does well in the redwood forest, where it can be found in the understory. Its range extends from British Columbia to the San Bernardino Mountains and to the Sierra Nevada.

You have probably also seen the dogwood used as an ornamental tree around homes. Be sure to let others know about its bark.

Western Redbud

On a springtime drive along Highway 20, I couldn't help but notice the beautiful purplish blossoms of the redbud. A small tree generally not more than 20-25 feet in height, redbud has a flush of striking magenta flowers in the spring. I remember as a student first seeing a redbud on a hot spring day.

Assuming that it was a non-native species planted for its lovely flowers, I thought that surely it required supplemental watering.

Not so. The tree is native and is wonderfully drought tolerant. Though you'd want to occasionally water a seedling planted in your garden during the first dry season or two, after that it requires no irrigation.

In addition to being a treat for the eyes, the flowers and even the young seedpods are edible. It's said that the early settlers used the blossoms as an addition to their salads. After flowering, redbud, which is a member of the pea family, forms numerous seedpods. These pods often form in thick clusters and hang on the tree, sometimes until the following spring.

The round leaves provide their own display of color in the fall. Depending on the temperature in the autumn, you might be treated to a show of scarlet, orange, or yellow leaves.

Known as western redbud or California redbud, the scientific name of this beautiful tree is *Cercis occidentalis*. The genus name, *Cercis*, comes from a Greek phrase meaning "weaver's shuttle." Perhaps this scientific name was given to the tree because of its extensive use by Native Americans in basket weaving. Branches were split into small, flexible strips and used for lovely reddish coloring.

A feast for the eyes in spring, naturally small in size and drought tolerant, this native tree is a real delight whether it is in the woods or in your garden.

The oldest trees--Bristlecone Pine

In 1999, the world's tallest tree, a 367-foot coast redwood, was recorded near Ukiah. Although the coast redwood is known for its longevity and ability to grow to great size, is not the oldest living tree. That distinction goes to the bristlecone pine.

The Great Basin bristlecone pines may reach 3000-5000 years of age. They occur in Inyo and Mono counties in California, as well as in Utah and Nevada. You might be surprised by the size of these trees-- bristlecone pines are generally under 40 feet tall and less than 5 feet in diameter!

The bristlecone pine grows at high elevations (5,500-11,650 feet, usually above 10,000 feet), and the oldest trees are found on the harshest sites. On the milder sites, the trees grow more quickly but also die sooner. This is because on milder sites, the increased moister and warmer temperatures create conditions in which there is more fuel for wildfires. There are also more bark beetles, fungi, and wildlife that can damage the trees and thus shorten its life span. The harsher bristlecone pine sites, which average only about 12 inches of precipitation each year, support fewer fungi and wildlife species and also produce less vegetation that can burn in a wildfire.

The average life expectancy of most California conifers is in the 300 to 500 year range. This is only about 1/10th the life span of the oldest bristlecone pines!

Tanoak

If you spend much time in the woods in our coastal forests, you know the tanoak tree, with its abundant acorn crop and dusty leaves that can make you sneeze. For years, tanoak has been considered by foresters as a troublesome weed species because it competes so successfully against conifer seedlings for light, water and nutrients. When cut, the tanoak sends out multiple sprouts from the stump. As with the stump sprouts of other hardwoods and redwoods, these sprouts feed off the well-established and extensive root system of the cut tree. While a planted conifer seedling might grow only several inches in the first year, it is not uncommon for stump sprouts to grow three feet or more in a single year. Uncontrolled, an opening quickly becomes a sea of tanoak sprouts, with planted trees struggling to survive.

This isn't to say that tanoak has no value. Wildlife utilize the acorns, and humans have long used the wood for firewood and the bark as a tannin source for tanning leather. Tanoak has also been one of the key species in the substantial effort to develop a hardwood industry in California. Years ago a tanoak floor was installed in the Mateel Community Center, and anyone who has seen that floor can attest to the beauty and durability of the wood. And the efforts continue with, for example, the Mendocino Redwood Company's effort to convert their sawmill in Willits to production of tanoak for flooring.

Whether the focus is on growing tanoaks or conifers, the plentiful and vigorous stump sprouts of the tanoak present a real challenge. The problem is that the stump sprouts are many in number, and from one stump, you might have a dozen sprouts. A couple of decades later, you have 6-10 sprouts per stump, each only a fraction of the diameter of the original tree. So instead of growing one 15-inch diameter tree that you might use for tanoak flooring, you end up with eight or ten 3-inch diameter stems that have no merchantable value, are of little use to wildlife, are stressed and provide an abundance of small diameter, relatively easily combustible material for a wildfire.

Although the tree is called tanoak, or tanbark oak, it is not really an oak. That designation has to do with plant taxonomy. Tanoaks are closely related to oaks (similarity seen in the acorns) as well as chestnuts (similarity seen in the flowers). But it belongs in a different genus named "*Lithocarpus*," meaning "stone fruit," a reference to the hard acorn. The tanoak usually grows 70-100 feet in height and 1-3 feet in diameter, though it can reach 150 feet and as much as 9 feet in diameter. The trees begin to produce seed after 30-40 years, and they can live 200-300 years or more.

Part II -- Understanding the Landscape

What's What?

What is an Acre?

An acre is the standard unit of area measurement in forestry, but what is it exactly? Mr. Webster defines an acre for us as a measure of land equal to 43,560 square feet. If an acre were perfectly square, it would work out to 208.7 feet on each side. Why is it such an odd size? It is based on the amount of land that a single able-bodied man was able to plow in a single day under typical conditions.

When trying to visualize large acreages, it is often helpful to think in terms of square miles. Each square mile contains 640 acres, making each 10,000 acres a little more than 15 square miles. So, for example, the 47,000-acre Storrie fire in the Sierras was about 73 square miles in size.

The acre is also the basis for another unit of linear measure used in forestry, the chain. One chain is equal to 66 feet, and it is the measure foresters and landowners use when talking of or pacing off distances in the woods. Conveniently, 10 square chains equals one acre.

The acre is laid out on maps and so is measured in what is known as horizontal distance, not slope distance. To understand the difference, think of a right triangle. The horizontal distance is the bottom leg of the triangle, and the slope distance is the longest leg (the hypotenuse). Unless you are on perfectly flat ground, your slope distance is always greater than your horizontal distance. So the steeper your ground, the more "extra" land you have.

If Monday night in the fall finds you watching the latest football game, probably the simplest way to think of an acre is to think of a football field, which is roughly an acre in size.

Large Woody Debris—What Is It and Why Should I Care?

As a young forester, my supervisor took me out to a harvest operation to look at logs in the watercourses. They were everywhere. He shook he head and commented, "Someday, you'll do it differently. There's a lot of good timber there just wasted." Well, foresters *do* do things differently today. But what we are doing differently is making *sure* that logs get into the watercourses, and that some remain in the woods.

It used to be standard practice to pull logs out of the watercourses. The thinking was that logs blocked fish passage and should be removed. But like the old policy of cutting all snags, we've found out that our good intentions ended up removing important wildlife habitat.

Woody debris is important for a number of reasons. For fish, it provides variation in the stream channel. A log may create a little waterfall that scours out a pool where fish can over-summer in the deep,

Pictured is a piece of suspended large woody debris (LWD) in a mixed conifer forest. It will be many years before this piece of LWD breaks down and becomes soil.

cool water. A log can also trap sediment, preventing its movement downstream and building up a step or even a gravel bar upstream. A log also traps leaves that decompose and become food for aquatic insects, which in turn are food for the fish. It also provides shadows in which small fish can hide from predators.

In the woods, large woody debris is important as wildlife habitat and as a way to recycle organic matter back into the forest floor. Logs can also help seedlings establish themselves, as they provide a bit of shade on hot days, and their cover of the soil helps keep soil moisture levels a little higher.

How "large" large woody debris needs to be depends on what biologist you are talking to, where you are, the wildlife species using the logs, and the tree species. Some biologists say you need a minimum of 2 pieces per acre at least 20" in diameter and 20 feet long. Your best bet is to aim for a diversity of sizes, species and stages of decay. As with so many other things in the forest, there is no magic "right"

This redwood log is left over from logging many years ago. The log is difficult to see because the leaves and other debris that have collected on top of it are decomposing and forming soil in which plants are starting to root.

number. The trick is to find balance. In this case it is balance between providing enough woody debris without creating too much fuel for wildfires.

I recently heard about a forest fire that started after someone had built their campfire against a log to help reflect the heat. It ended up smoldered for days before finally breaking out in a wildfire. So if you want to use your forest's woody debris for a fire, put it inside your woodstove first! And don't forget to leave some out in the woods.

What *Is* Old Growth, Anyway?

In March of 2000 I picked up a fact sheet at a CDF office in Sacramento. That sheet told me that there were about 133,513 acres of "old growth" in California. Some 15% were under private ownership, 60% in redwood parks, and the remaining 25% on federal lands. I assume this sheet was referring to old-growth redwood and other conifer forests, but it begs the question, just what *is* old growth?

I remember doing a radio interview in which the interviewer kept coming around to the question, "How old does a tree have to be before it's considered old-growth?" That question missed a key point—old growth refers to an ecosystem, not to an individual tree. An individual tree may be very old, but it takes many old trees to make an old-growth forest. Like an individual, a forest and its trees go through stages of development: establishment ("birth," if you will), juvenile, early mature, mid-mature, late-mature, and finally old-growth.

Remember that old growth is not limited to redwoods. If redwood is the climax species, then you will have a redwood old-growth forest. But in other areas, you might have a mixed-conifer or Douglas-fir old-growth forest. Foresters even joke about "old-growth manzanita." The key is not a particular species or a particular age, but the relative age and functional characteristics of the ecosystem.

A multitude of characteristics distinguish an old growth forest from a forest of a younger seral (development) stage. The ***Dictionary of Forestry*** outlines these characteristics quite well. Some include: number and size of climax trees, whether or not there are trees that are large for their species, canopy conditions and complexity, number and size of snags as well as large woody debris. It also states that "(stand) age, although a useful indicator of old growth, is often considered less important than structure…"

And how big does a forest have to be to function as old growth? It depends on what species you are talking about, where you are in the range of that species, site quality, etc. Ultimately the question is, how much land is needed for the forest to function as old growth? While it is true that areas that are too small will not have the space needed to develop the characteristics of an old-growth forest, there is no magical minimum acreage.

We live in a society where we want exact answers to our questions. Forestry tends to be amazingly site specific and species specific, however, and it simply does not lend itself well to broad-brush generalization. What is old growth? As in so many other areas of forestry, the answer is exceedingly simply and exceedingly complicated: it depends.

Preservation & Conservation – What's the Difference?

There is a difference between preservation and conservation. Preservation calls for a hands-off approach, allowing for no management. Typically what will be set aside for preservation is determined by an easily identified characteristic, such as everything within a certain distance from a watercourse or the diameter of a tree. If a stand or a tree meets the prescribed criteria, it can't be managed now or in the future.

An important shortcoming of preservation is that it makes no provision for changes over time. This is critical when dealing with forests whose health depends on fires in a time when we suppress wildfires. A no-management policy approach can lead to problems in forest health due to overcrowding and stress. It can also create an inability to effectively respond to events like insect infestations or disease.

Conservation is a different kind of approach, one in which management is permitted. Under a conservation approach to forest management, resource professionals look at factors like changes over time, resiliency of the stand, the stand to be left after harvest, and the fertility of the site. The goal is to provide for a sustainable system in terms of the resources while also providing for compatible human and wildlife uses.

A shortcoming of the conservation approach is that it assumes that the (human) parties involved can find common ground and have a certain level of trust. When there is disagreement about what the goals should be or what sustainability means, or if the parties involved distrust one another, it becomes difficult if not impossible to come up with an appropriate management strategy.

To advocate preservation is to move to ban management. To advocate conservation is to move to provide clarification as to what the goals are (fuel reduction, timber production, wildlife habitat management, good aesthetics, etc.) and then to actively work toward those goals.

It's worth remembering that we in California currently harvest less than 30% of the wood we use in the state. Preserving more trees here at home means meeting even more of our demand through imports. If we as a public do decide to preserve more forestland, we need to take responsibility for the ecological and ethical implications of relying even more heavily on wood from forests that are less well protected than our own.

Rotation Ages

A common term in forestry is "rotation age," which refers to the length of time between when a forest is established (for example by planting) and when it is harvested. This is a term used in even-aged management, in which most of the trees are roughly the same age. Under even-aged management, most or all of the overstory trees outside of protected areas such as riparian zones are harvested, allowing a new age class of trees to grow and, at the designated rotation age, be harvested. This is in contrast to what is called uneven-aged management, in which there are several different age classes of trees and only a few trees are removed at any one time. Under uneven-aged management, talking about a rotation age wouldn't make any sense, since most of the trees remain standing.

On nearly all of California's private forest lands, the minimum rotation age is 80 years for less fertile lands and 60 years for more fertile lands. That means before a stand of trees can be cut, the minimum age, which is based on site class, for the stand must be met. The relatively long minimum rotation allows for diversity to develop within the stand, in terms of structure, vegetation and wildlife habitat. Those who want to maximize economic returns would argue that the minimum rotation age is too long. Those who want to grow wildlife habitat for species that use older forests would argue the minimum age is too short. But the standard, set by the state years ago, is what we have to work with.

Other states and other countries have different standards. Some have no standards at all. When I worked on a forestry job in two southeastern states, I was very surprised to see that foresters and landowners in the southeast were harvesting trees at rotation ages of only 15 to 25 years. In all fairness, it must be pointed out that those pines harvested after such a short time have a natural life span that is shorter than our west coast species such as ponderosa pine, sugar pine, or Douglas fir. Still, to a forester from the west coast, the rotation ages seemed very short indeed.

Snags

Do you know what a standing dead tree is called? It's referred to as a "snag." A forest should have a good diversity of snags--some conifer, some hardwood, some large diameter, some in early decay classes, and some in later decay classes. While having some snags is beneficial, having too many reduces the level of forest health. When a forest fire sweeps through, snags become a source of very dry fuel that feeds the fire.

Not all snags are alike. Two important ways in which they differ are "decay class" and diameter. A snag takes many years to completely decay, and the stages of decay are often referred to as decay classes. In the early stages, the snag will be very hard, and it will still have all or some of its bark. In later stages, the bark falls off, and the snag becomes soft. Snags with large diameters are useful because they can provide habitat for species that are physically large. These snags also take longer to decay.

Many wildlife species use snags, each a little differently. If you look closely at a snag, you will see the various habitat components it provides. Where the bark has become loose, you may find insects in the crevices. This thin space is also a favorite place of bats. You may also notice cavities, typically created by woodpeckers. Woodpeckers are "primary cavity nesters," meaning they create their own cavities. There are also "secondary cavity nesters" who use abandoned or natural cavities.

Like many things in the forest, snags are most beneficial when they are diverse and in balance--not too many, not too few.

Shaded Fuelbreaks

As its name implies, a fuelbreak provides a break in the continuity of fuels. It might be a block or strip of land in which brush and other vegetation is entirely or partially removed. The idea is to significantly reduce the available fuels so that when a wildfire comes through, the amount of available fuel for the fire is significantly reduced, which reduces the intensity of the fire.

Fuelbreaks are strategically placed in locations where firefighters will have good access and where natural and human-made features will help them fight the fire. Often they are put on top of ridges. Or they may be placed next to roads, with vegetation reduced in strips 30 feet wide or more along either or both sides of the road.

Many people think of fuelbreaks as strips of land cut down to the ground, with nothing growing in them. But these days many communities are establishing "shaded fuelbreaks." In these areas, brush such as manzanita and ceanothus is controlled, and trees are thinned. A rule of thumb for thinning trees in fuelbreaks is dbh+4+1/3. Take the diameter of the tree in inches, add 4, then multiply by 1.33 to get the spacing of leave trees in feet. So between 11-inch diameter trees, you would want a spacing of 20 feet. Usually the lower limbs on remaining trees are removed so that fire cannot climb up into the tree canopy. What is left is a widely spaced stand of overstory trees over an understory that has been largely cleared of brush.

Above shows an area in Yuba County without a shaded fuelbreak. Below is an adjacent property of the same timber type with a shaded fuelbreak.

Experience has shown that these shaded fuelbreaks are effective in slowing wildfires, particularly on gentle slopes. A forester in the Sierras recently told a story about a wildfire that was moving in the tree canopy and hit a shaded fuel break. The fire dropped to the ground and burned through, leaving the overstory trees with some char marks on their bark but otherwise in good shape. When the fire left the fuelbreak area, it climbed back up into the canopy.

What is Sustainability?

Many people talk about the goal of having sustainable forests. But what *is* sustainability? "Sustainability" basically means keeping a system functioning well in the long term. This includes maintaining health, diversity, productivity, as well as the overall integrity of the biological system. We can talk about the sustainability of a stand of trees, an entire forest, or an entire biome, but the basic principles are the same: keep the resources healthy, productive, and diverse.

In our Western forests, fire is an integral part of our forests. When we exclude fire to protect our human interests, we interfere with the sustainability of the forest. The absence of fire leads to an immense build-up of fuels, not to mention overcrowding and stress that make the trees more susceptible to attack by disease and insects.

How do we know if we've achieved sustainability? First, we look at the overall health of the forest. We want individual trees that are vigorous and not competing with excessive neighboring vegetation. We also want good seed sources for the next generation of trees.

Second, we look at the forest's productivity. A sustainable forest grows as much or more wood as is harvested while protecting critical resources like soil and water. Maintaining long-term productivity means taking measures to minimize erosion and soil compaction, and to ensure well-functioning streams. It also means finding the funds to pay for work needed to restore, maintain, and monitor.

Third, we look at the level of diversity. The key is to provide a balance of forest types and ages. Different plant and animal species have very different requirements. Some need young forests, others prefer brush, others rely on old growth, and still others require grassland and mature trees. An over-emphasis on one habitat type can lead to a lot of habitat for certain species at the expense of others.

When thinking about sustainability, it's useful to look both at individual stands and the larger landscape level. But regardless of whether we are considering a single stand or an entire landscape, an intensively managed or unmanaged forest, a sustainable system is one that is healthy, productive, and diverse.

What is Silviculture?

"Silviculture" is a cornerstone of the forestry profession, but what exactly is it? The word "silviculture" comes from two Latin root words: "silva," meaning "forest" or "woodlands," and "cultus," meaning "cultivation." Literally translated, silviculture is the cultivation of the forest. Within the forestry profession, silviculture is commonly defined as the art and science of growing trees to meet the owner's management objectives.

Silviculture is a science because it relies upon a body of research having to do with how trees grow, both individually and relative to each other in the context of various management frameworks such as a stand or a watershed. A forester's scientific training that is put to use in the practice of silviculture includes plant biology, forest ecology, soil science, entomology, pathology, and genetics to name a few.

Silviculture is an art because the knowledge gained from science must be put into practice in the field, where nature is highly variable. When we try to come up with broad generalizations in the forest, we constantly find exceptions. The forester considers parameters like the forest type, elevation, slope, aspect, soil type, weather patterns, rainfall and snowfall patterns, etc. when making silvicultural decisions. The art is in the exercise of professional judgment.

A forester is constantly refining his or her craft through experience and observation. "Cookbook" approaches do not work well, for the practice of good silvicultural needs to be based on an understanding of science at work in the woods as well as the ability to apply that science in ways that make sense in the real world.

What is a Watershed?

There is a lot of talk about watersheds these days. Some schools are using the "Adopt-A-Watershed" curriculum, and in communities local watershed groups are being formed. But just what is a watershed?

A watershed is simply an area of land from which all the water flows into a particular creek, river, or other body of water. So watershed boundaries follow ridgelines. Use your hand to illustrate this. Cup your hand and hold it out under dripping water. The water that hits the "ridgeline" of your hand and runs down into your palm is flowing into your "watershed."

You can talk about a watershed for a small creek where the watershed might be tens or hundreds of acres, or for a large river like the Eel where the watershed is many thousands of acres. Watersheds can also overlap. The watershed for Rattlesnake Creek or one of its tributaries, for example, is different from the watershed for Ten Mile Creek. But since they both flow into the South Fork of the Eel River, they are both part of the South Fork watershed.

The amount of runoff within a watershed is determined by several factors, the most important being the size of the watershed, vegetation type, and the amount of precipitation, either as rain or snow. It is mandatory for foresters to consider impacts on watersheds when planning forest management activities today, and an important part of the planning process is a watershed assessment.

Not all of the water that falls on a watershed ends up leaving the watershed as runoff. The trees and other plants in the watershed pump water out of the soil, evaporating it into the air in a process called evapotranspiration. The annual amount of water leaving a drainage basin varies from less than 10% in hot chaparral areas to 50% in mixed conifer forests.

Pictured is the mouth of the Klamath River in Del Norte County. The Klamath River watershed encompasses approximately 10 million acres, according to the US Fish & Wildlife Service.

Succession

The holidays in 2000 found me driving through Canada's southern Ontario with its miles and miles of woods. The deep snow, freezing weather, granite boulders, and occasional moose differed from the forests of home, but the vast expanses of wooded land were similar. Driving along these heavily forested roads, I was struck by the clear, textbook-like examples of succession along the roadsides.

A forest is made up of trees. Succession refers to how those trees change over time. Take a major event, like a landslide or a catastrophic fire, that removes all the vegetation from an area. At first, you might have only brush growing and occupying the space. These are the "pioneer" species. They provide shade, slope stability, and even changes in the soil (like fixing nitrogen) that allow for other species to come in. After the pioneer species, often hardwood trees become a second "successional stage." They create small climatic changes that allow for conifers to become established, creating the next successional stage. In some forests, certain conifer species create conditions that allow for yet another successional stage of different conifers species that require a lot of shade. Finally, this process of succession creates what is known as a "climax forest" or "climax stage."

Along the highways of Canada, there were miles and miles of hardwood forests (such as birch and poplar) with the dark green of conifers (spruce and balsam fir) underneath. The hardwoods were old and had provided shade that allowed the conifers to establish themselves over the 10-30 years. The conifers were fighting their way up to the sun, and as the hardwoods died and fell over, more light was able to get the conifers, allowing them to grow more quickly. In several decades, one will be able to drive those highways and see conifer forests with a few scattered hardwoods.

As in so many aspects of forestry, the specifics vary from region to region, but the general principles are the same. In our neck of the woods, we can most easily see succession at work in some of our hardwood woodlands, like oak or tanoak. The hardwoods act as a "nurse" crop for the conifers, most typically Douglas-fir. For several decades the Douglas-fir fights its way to the top of the oaks. When it succeeds, it begins to shade out the oaks. Eventually the oaks will die, and the conifers will become the dominant species.

All this happens over a very long time scale, ranging from decades to hundreds of years. Sometime we try to speed up succession through actions like planting after fires, or harvesting hardwoods and releasing the native conifers underneath. Understanding and working with these natural processes is an important component of good forest management.

This oak tree is acting as a nurse tree for the small Douglas-fir seedlings in the foreground of this photo.

What is Tolerance?

One of the driving forces behind succession is the concept of "tolerance," or "shade tolerance." A shade-tolerant plant is one that does well without a lot of direct sunlight. White fir is a good example of a shade-tolerant tree species. "Shade-intolerant" plants do much better with direct sunlight, and lots of it. Ponderosa pine and sugar pine, for example, are very shade-intolerant trees. Some species are intermediates, and some can act as shade tolerants or shade intolerants depending on the local climate. Douglas-fir is a good example of an intermediate tree.

In the early successional stages, there is little or no shade available, so shade-intolerant plants move in. But they may create enough shade so that they cannot reproduce very well, and more shade-tolerant plants become established. In later successional stages, there is shade everywhere, and only shade-tolerant plants can successfully reproduce.

You might think that the entire landscape would eventually go to shade-intolerant species, but in fact that is not what is supposed to happen. Historically, fire and landslides created openings and started the cycle of succession all over again, or kicked things back a successional stage or two. For example, a low-intensity fire going through a mature Ponderosa pine stand would kill the saplings and seedlings of more shade tolerant conifers while leaving the large Ponderosa pine alive and well.

Since we have suppressed fire so successfully, we have found that the result is forests with an increasing number of shade-tolerant trees. Whether or not this is a problem depends on your perspective, but the fact is that the intervention of humans has had and continues to have a significant impact on the composition of the forest in many ways. The species shift to shade intolerant trees is just one example.

What is a Forester?

Many people think of foresters as park rangers, while others are not quite sure what a forester is. A question I often hear is, "Oh, you're a forester. What exactly is a forester? What do you do?"

Foresters are basically land and vegetation managers who actively work with those resources to achieve the landowners' objectives within the applicable laws, whether they work for a public agency, a private company, as private consultants, or an educational institution. Most foresters have either a 2-year or 4-year forestry degree from a Society of American Foresters-accredited college or university. Graduates choose one of several general career paths: field forestry (active land management), recreation, office specialties (planning, computer work, etc.), or academia (teaching and research).

Foresters who work for private landowners, whether industrial firms with thousands of acres or small private landowners, are involved in activities such as inventory, Timber Harvest Plan preparation, harvesting operations, appraisal, and reforestation. These foresters are generally Registered Professional Foresters (RPFs).

Foresters who work for the California Department of Forestry & Fire Protection may be involved in fire control, enforcement of the state forest practice rules on private land, or the management of one of the State's Demonstration Forests.

Foresters who work for public agencies such as the Forest Service or the Bureau of Land Management may be involved in specialized fields or general land management. Federal foresters are often responsible for administering and managing activities on thousands of acres of publicly owned forests. They may monitor forest conditions, conduct wildlife studies, plan land management plan activities, prepare and supervise timber sales, manage wilderness areas or work in fire control.

A Registered Professional Forester inspects a watercourse crossing that was pulled after a logging operation was completed.

Most foresters spend a lot of time in the field in addition to countless hours doing paperwork. One thing they all share is the concern and love for the forest that drew them into the field in the first place.

What is an RPF?

All RPFs are foresters, but not all foresters are RPFs. In order to practice forestry on private land in California, a forester must be licensed by the state as an RPF, a Registered Professional Forester. To obtain a license, a forester must have a combination of seven years of qualifying education and/or experience before taking the licensing exam. A Bachelor of Science degree counts for four years out of the seven needed.

36

The licensing exam is seven hours of essay and short answer questions, covering a broad range of topics within the field from forest practice rules to forest ecology to forest engineering. The pass rate is about 20 to 40 percent, which reflects the difficulty of the test and the high standards that must be met by practicing professionals. When a forester passes the test, he or she becomes a Registered Professional Forester, or RPF for short.

An RPF can practice forestry on private land in the state, subject to the Forest Practices Act and the rules and regulations enforced by the CDF. Basically, this means that RPFs are the only ones who can prepare and submit timber harvest plans and other management plans allowed under the Forest Practice Act. Foresters have been licensed in California since the mid-1970s, and about 2800 RPF licenses have been issued, although not all of these are active.

Foresters who work for federal agencies do not need to be state-licensed to work on federal land, although many are. They do, however, go through a federal certification process in order to practice in their area of specialty.

An Introduction to the THP and NTMP

If you are doing any commercial harvesting of your trees in California, you need a management plan, usually a Timber Harvest Plan (THP) or Non-industrial Timber Management Plan (NTMP), that is approved by the California Department of Forestry (CDF). This is true whether you plan to sell the logs or just want to trade them with someone. THPs and NTMPS also fulfill the California Environmental Quality Act (CEQA) mandate that projects, such as commercial timber management, consider a broad range of potential impacts.

There are a few important differences between a THP and an NTMP. First, a THP is valid for three years plus a maximum of two one-year extensions, whereas an approved NTMP is valid in perpetuity. Second, an NTMP requires a cruise and a growth and yield analysis to demonstrate that harvests will not exceed growth for each 10-year period, so it is more expensive than a THP. Third, NTMPs must use uneven-aged silviculture, while either even-aged or uneven-aged systems can be used under a THP.

The document normally required to fulfill CEQA is an Environmental Impact Report (EIR). A THP or NTMP, however, has been determined in the state court system to be the *functional equivalent* of an EIR, thus fulfilling CEQA requirements. The detailed information required by the California Forest Practice Rules in THPs and NTMPs is necessary to meet CEQA, the Federal Endangered Species Act, and a host of other state and federal laws designed to protect the environment.

To write a typical THP or NTMP, a lot of fieldwork has to be done, as you would expect. But you may be surprised by how much office work is required. While plans twenty years ago may have been only a few pages, today (1999) plans are typically 100 pages or more and takes months to prepare. *(Note: Since 1999, increasing plan complexity has meant that it is not unusual to have 200 page plans.)*

What kind of office work does the Registered Professional Forester who prepares the plan have to do? In addition to making detailed maps and written plans about the trees and roads, he or she notifies the public, local Native American tribes, neighbors, etc. of the proposed activities. The RPF also addresses concerns relating to wildlife, archaeology, erosion, protection of riparian areas, and silviculture. Plans are public records, so if you are curious, visit the local CDF office and ask to see a plan. You'll be amazed by what it covers.

Licensed Timber Operators (LTOs)

A landowner asked me how he could get the training needed to do the logging on his own property. He has had a timber harvest plan written for his parcel and wants to start the logging next year. He is aware that in California, this work needs to be done by a Licensed Timber Operator (LTO) who is licensed by the state. But instead of hiring an independent LTO, this landowner would much rather do the work himself.

The licensing of timber operators is covered under the Forest Practices Act. A Licensed Timber Operator is required if there will be commercial cutting or removal or sawlogs, veneer log, pulp logs, poles or piling. An LTO is also required for work such as certain kinds of site preparation (in preparation for planting).

The California Department of Forestry and Fire Protection works with three colleges in the state to offer classes on Timber Operator Training. A landowner who will work only on his or her own property is eligible to take this class to become an LTO. Others must have several thousand hours of qualifying experience, as defined in the Forest Practice Rules, to apply for the license.

Timber Operator Training classes are generally held on weekends. They are offered through Mendocino Community College, Sierra College, and College of the Siskiyous. For more information, call the Forest Stewardship Helpline at 800-738-8733 or CDF at 916-653-7211.

The Forest Practice Rules (FPR)

A fellow from Idaho who had recently purchased forestland in California called my office to find out about harvesting timber from his land. He was surprised to find out that California has Forest Practice Rules. I didn't have the heart to tell him he had just purchased land in the state with the toughest forest practice rules in the country.

In fact, many people think our forest practice rules in California are the toughest in the world. Some states don't have forest practice rules at all. The author of an article in a forestry newsletter from back east lamented the fact that well over 50% of the landowners who logged their forests did not even involve a forester, let alone have a forester come up with a written management plan.

The Rules for California were first adopted after the Forest Practices Act was passed in 1973. The Act gave the Board of Forestry the authority to adopt rules that are designed to foster production of high-quality timber products while maintaining biological diversity and watershed integrity.

Recognizing the variation in forest types and growth habits, the Rules divide the state up into three forest districts, with slight variations of rules for each district. In 1999, there were 235 pages of rules, covering silviculture and post-harvest stocking standards, harvesting practices, erosion control, protection of watercourses and lakes, site preparation, wildlife protection, fire protection, hazard reduction, archaeological resources, conversion, and a lot more.

You can download of the current Forest Practice Rules from the CDF website, http://www.fire.ca.gov. Or stop by your local CDF station and pick up a paper copy for $5.

The Board of Forestry (BOF)

California's Board of Forestry & Fire Protection is the body that licenses the state's professional foresters (RPFs), considers changes to the Forest Practice Rules, and develops general forest policy for the state.

The board has been around since 1885, and its members have always been appointed by the governor. Of course, when the governor doesn't appoint enough members to achieve a quorum (as happened under Gray Davis), the board cannot conduct business.

There are nine seats on the board. Four are filled by members of the public, three by members of the forest products industry, and one member represents range and livestock concerns. The board is very powerful because it is the body that considers and makes changes to the Forest Practice Rules. The rules govern harvest of timber on private lands as well as the registration requirements for professional foresters. Some of the changes made are minor in nature. Some of the changes dramatically alter forestry in California by introducing new or expanded requirements.

The changes to the rules being proposed at any given time are posted on the internet on the Board's website under "Proposed Rule Package." If you feel strongly about an issue, you can send in written comments, or you can personally attend a meeting and address the board during the "Public Forum."

Board meetings are held every month. Meetings are often in Sacramento, but the board does travel around the state for quite a few meetings each year so they can arrange field trips and see what is happening on the ground. Agendas are available on the website or by calling the Board of Forestry office at 916-653-8007.

Information & Issues for Forest Landowners

Certification

You may have heard something about "certified" lumber or wood, but what exactly does that mean? Like "organic" produce, "certified" lumber indicates to the consumer something about the processes that were and were not used to get that item to the store shelf. "Certification" is designed to assure the consumer that the wood product in the store came from a log that was harvested in an ecologically well-managed forest.

Certification is typically done by a third party, so it is sometimes called "third-party certification." This means that it's not enough for the landowner, the forester, or the mill to say their own practices are ecologically sound. Rather, a third party without a direct economic interest has to determine the practices are appropriate.

There are several organizations doing certification in California. Some of the certifiers you might hear about on the north coast are SmartWood (www.smartwood.org) and Scientific Certification Systems (www.scs1.com), who both offer certification through the Forest Stewardship Council. A competing certification is that offered by SFI, the Sustainable Forestry Initiative. In my experience, most small landowners and private foresters who want to be certified opt for FSC, while industrial owners may favor SFI. Other certifications are offered by the American Tree Farm System (www.treefarmsystem.org) and Green Tag Forestry.

Each group has its own set of standards, its own method of developing standards, and its own certifiers who go out in the field to review on-the-ground practices. Most certification standards relate to practices out in the woods--silviculture, protection of watercourses and wildlife habitat, road maintenance, etc. But some standards, notably FSC, look at how the local human community is impacted by harvesting by asking questions about worker safety, creation of local jobs, etc. Mills are also certified to ensure lumber sold as certified came from logs harvested under certified forestry practices.

All these standards mean more work and expense for the forester and the logger, so you can expect the cost of certified lumber to be higher. Certification is already big in Europe and is catching hold here in the US with big retailers like Home Depot. Next time you shop for a 2x4, you might look to see if the retailer carries any certified lumber.

More on Certification

Most people would agree that it would be a fairly remarkable achievement to bring together and find common ground between representatives from environmental organizations like the Sierra Club, Greenpeace, or the Wilderness Society and people who are interested in logging their lands, be they small private landowners or large companies. The Forest Stewardship Council is just such an organization. And the issue that has brought these diverse stakeholders to the table is certification, or verification of good forest management operations.

Since 1993 the Forest Stewardship Council (FSC) has been working with these groups on hammering out Guidelines for economically, ecologically and socially sound and practical forest management. The process has frequently been described as difficult and intense, but the result is that both forestry interests and environmental interests support the Guidelines. That is a powerful combination.

The Guidelines can be applied anywhere and examine the management and results of management in three areas: ecological, economic, and social. Local and regional resource managers and other experts form a team that uses the Guidelines in reviewing and assessing whether or not a certain forester or forest operation should be granted certification status and thereby allowed to use the FSC logo. Continued adherence to the Guidelines is verified through annual audits of the forest management practices.

There has been a surge of interest in FSC certification, and since 1999 the amount of FSC-certified land in the US has doubled to a level of 8-9 million acres. As of 2001, about 10% of that acreage was in California. Big retailers like Home Depot and Lowe's have said that they are moving toward replacing non-certified wood products with certified products. The big question is, since good management costs the landowner more money, will the retailers be willing to pay more for certified wood products? More to the point, will consumers be willing to pay more? Will you?

Conservation Easements – Proceed with Caution

The conservation easement is a clever tool that works well to limit human activity on private property. But like any tool, it must be used wisely. Whenever forest land is involved, a landowner should have a trusted and experienced forester review an easement before it is signed.

The conservation easement is designed as a legal way for landowners to give up rights they don't intend to use in return for a nice income tax deduction. For example, a forest might have a lot of value because its soil would be terrific for vineyards. But if the landowner wants to make sure that vineyards are never put in, she can have a conservation easement written to permanently relinquish that right.

If the property were worth $300,000 with the right to develop vineyards but only $275,000 without that right, the landowner would get a tax deduction of $25,000. Though the deduction can be spread out over several years, clearly easements only work if you have a lot of income and can use that much of a tax deduction.

A landowner can give up as many or as few rights as she wants, and there is a lot of room for creativity. For example, I know of a landowner who wanted to manage timber on a 100-year rotation, significantly longer than what is required by law. By writing the longer management timeframe into the easement, he was able to get a bigger tax deduction.

The reason to be cautious, however, is that is easy for landowners to give up more rights than intended. Blanket statements have the potential to trip up landowners years later when there are unforeseen circumstances. For example, a prohibition on all logging may backfire when a landowner wants to manage timber for fire risk reduction, take out dead trees after a fire or insect attack, or to clear an area for a new road or homesite.

Conservation easements are excellent tools, but they not forgiving. They stand as legal documents, unforeseen circumstances or not. So landowners should carefully consider what rights they are relinquishing when writing an easement. And when forest land is involved, landowners will find it a wise choice to consult a forester who can explain the intended as well as the potential unintended consequences of the easement.

Forest Legacy

Forest Legacy is a federal program designed to help landowners put conservation easements on their properties. It promotes working forests and putting easements on forests that are at high risk of being developed.

A popular misconception about conservation easements is that they lock up your land so that you can't manage it. That's not the case. Of course if you want to, you can write conservation easements to be very restrictive. But you can just as easily give up some rights--for example the right to subdivide or to put in vineyards—while retaining others, such as timber harvesting rights. Or you could give up the right to harvest timber on 60-year rotations and instead lock the property into 100-year minimum rotations. The easement can be as restrictive or as non-restrictive as you want it to be.

The Forest Legacy program is designed to help keep working forestland intact by putting conservation easements on forests in areas at risk of being developed.

Legacy helps cover the costs of writing, recording and putting in place the easement, which can be substantial. But it also can reimburse landowners for the monetary value given up in the easement. Here's an example. Owners of one property of over 400 acres in Sonoma County put in an easement to give up vineyard development rights on 120 acres. The value of what they are giving up is an estimated $1.5 million, and they are applying to Legacy for $500,000.

The program is fairly competitive, but the rewards are substantial if your project is selected. If you would like to find out more about the Forest Legacy Program and if your property might qualify, contact Jeff Calvert at the California Department of Forestry at jeff_calvert@fire.ca.gov or 916-653-8286.

Forest Management for the Uninterested

There is an increasing number of forest landowners in California who either can't afford or don't have any interest in commercial timber harvesting. One reason is the skyrocketing cost of complying with a nightmarish maze of regulations. Another reason is that people are buying forest lands for private retreats where aesthetic enjoyment becomes their most highly valued land use.

Many "private retreat" landowners will say they aren't especially interested in managing their forest. Then, without realizing the implication that some kind of management is in fact needed, many will say that they want to do what they need to in order to keep their forest healthy.

It's important to remember that even when commercial harvesting isn't being done, forests require regular maintenance. The notion of "letting nature take its course" is fine if you don't mind your house burning up in a fire or unmaintained roads dumping sediment into watercourses, but for most of us, those aren't the preferred alternatives.

What kind of maintenance is needed? At the top of the list are management of roads and vegetation. Roads require annual maintenance. That means fixing obvious trouble spots and keeping an eye on the roads, particularly during the winter. Problems do develop – culverts plug up, water erodes the edges of the road, gullies form, etc. No problem is too small, as minor problems have a way of becoming major repairs if not tended to early.

Second is the management of vegetation. Exactly what form that should take of course depends on the objectives of the owner, but reduction of fuels to reduce the chance of a catastrophic fire is almost always a very good place to start.

Just as we maintain our houses to keep them in good working order and tend our gardens to keep them healthy and productive, we need to maintain our forests as well.

Forests, Harvests and Taxes

It is not at all uncommon for forest landowners to look to timber harvesting to help pay the costs of maintaining their property. Road maintenance and property taxes are arguably the most significant such cost. In addition to property tax, landowners find themselves paying yield tax, income tax, and inheritance tax.

Property tax is of course something that comes around every year. The amount varies depending on factors such as the acreage of the property and its zoning. The timber itself is not taxed until it is harvested.

When the timber is harvested, California's Timber Yield Tax kicks in. This tax is based on the volume and the species harvested. The Timber Yield Tax applies to any commercial species harvested, including both hardwoods and softwoods.

The profit to a landowner from harvesting is of course taxable as income. The IRS has published a book, the ***Forest Owners' Guide to the Federal Income Tax***. It's a few years old but packed with good information—probably more than you really ever wanted to know on the subject.

But the hardest-hitting tax comes when the younger generation inherits the lands and is faced with estate taxes. Often the land is valuable enough and the cash resources of the family small enough that paying estate taxes proves very difficult. Some families can generate the needed cash through harvesting, but sometimes family assets, even the land itself, end up being sold. Estate planning is a very complicated business but can go a long way to keeping family lands intact.

Call the Forest Stewardship Helpline, 800-738-8733, for information on the IRS publication as well as a free copy of the brochure explaining the Timber Yield Tax.

Tax Time for Forest Landowners

As tax time descends upon us each April, it's a good idea for forest landowners to review special situations that may help in reducing the size of the check to Uncle Sam.

For example, forest landowners who planted trees are generally eligible for a federal tax credit. For the first $10,000 you spend, you can claim a 10% credit (that's a *credit*, which is a much better deal than a deduction). So if you spend $4,000 on reforestation, you can take a $400 tax credit for the year in which you had the expenses.

Another great tax benefit is that you can deduct 95% of the reforestation expenses over 7 years. Again, if you spend $4,000, you deduct a total of $3,800, which works out to a little more than $500 per year.

You can also deduct costs for management and maintenance of existing timber stands, but usually this is done for the year you have expenses, rather than over the 7-year period used for reforestation expenses. Also, if your timber was damaged by wildfire or storms, you may qualify to take a "casualty loss."

Some landowners receive cost-share payments for tree planting and other activities through programs like CFIP, FIP or EQIP. These payments have to be reported. You might be able to exclude some of it, but it all has to be reported.

If you sold timber, it is better to report income from the sale as capital gains, rather than as ordinary income. You can do this if you held the timber for at least 12 months. The advantage is that this way you will probably pay a lower rate and will avoid having to pay the 15% self-employment tax on that money.

The Forest Service publishes a 2-page summary of *Tax Tips for Forest Landowners* each year. For a copy of this year's *Tax Tips,* call the Forest Stewardship Helpline at 800-738-8733.

The Global Climate Exchange (CCX)

When in the autumn of 2002 I heard on the radio a news report about the opening of the Chicago Climate Exchange, I thought I'd heard it wrong. But the announcer said it again a several times, adding details about the trade of carbon credits. With a Climate Exchange Website now on the internet, there can be no mistake that this exchange has indeed been established.

Yes, folks, this is trading in emissions, a voluntary "cap-and-trade" program. Companies will be able to get credits for reducing emissions or for projects that offset emissions. One example of an offset might be establishing a forest carbon sink (where carbon is stored in solid form as wood). The credits can then be sold to companies that have exceeded their cap.

How are the caps set? Baseline data was taken from 1998-2001, and the goal is to reduce emissions by 4% by the year 2006. While the commitment made by the participating companies is voluntary, it is legally binding. There are some heavy hitters behind this exchange, including Ford Motor Company, Waste Management, Inc., and Motorola. Trading is to cover credits for six greenhouse gases including carbon dioxide (CO_2) and sulphur dioxide (SO_2).

This is something for forest landowners to keep an eye on. Since forests are carbon sinks, the potential is there for forest landowners or their representatives to become traders in carbon credits. It may be some time before we get to that point, but for now, put the Climate Exchange on your radar screen.

For a list of participating companies or other information, visit the Global Climate Exchange (CCX) website at www.chicagoclimatex.com.

Tick Time

After a hike in the woods one day in May, I spotted a small tick on my arm. Grabbing the body of the tick, I pulled straight back, and the head of the tick came out cleanly with a small clicking sound. Since then I've been watching the area of the bite for any signs of redness that could indicate Lyme disease.

Lyme disease is carried by the deer tick, a small dark tick. There's a larger tick, lighter brown in color with a whitish curve on its back a little like a crescent moon, that is common in our woods but is not a carrier of Lyme disease. If you are bitten by a tick and aren't sure if it's a deer tick or not, the simplest thing to do is put it in a jar and pop it in the freezer for identification later by someone who knows their ticks.

If you are bitten, get the tick out as soon as possible. It takes as long as eight hours for a deer tick to transmit Lyme disease to a person, so if you are bitten and get the tick out within a few hours, you should be fine whether or not the tick was a carrier. To remove the tick, grab the body and pull straight out. If you twist the body, you risk breaking off the tick's head while it is still imbedded in you.

If you were bitten and the tick was in you for eight hours or more before you found it, watch for the physical signs of Lyme disease. Most people have heard about a bull's-eye ring that forms around the site of the bite, but the redness can take many forms. It may be nothing more than a red dot the size of the tip of your pinkie at the site of the bite. If you have redness that persists for many days, see your doctor and get it checked out.

Finally, do what you can to avoid tick bites in the first place. Wear long-sleeved shirts and pants, try not to brush up against bushes or bushy trees, and check yourself over carefully after a hike. The best way to check is to take a shower and change your clothes after you get home. I've noticed that ticks are often very active on sunny, warm days following periods of rain, so be especially careful on those days.

Management Tools

Forest Stewardship Plans – Implementing Good Intentions

Many of us know from experience that we are more likely to do something and do it well if we plan for it. This is true in part because planning gets us thinking and directing our attention to our goals, and in part because planning helps us clarify specific goals and the concrete steps we need to take to meet them.

Forest management is no exception to this rule. For landowners who harvest commercially, detailed planning is a built-in requirement of doing harvesting in California (that's not so in some other states). But for others whose primary value for their forest is aesthetics, fuels management, providing good wildlife habitat, etc. the importance of having a plan is easily overlooked.

A stewardship plan is designed to help a forest landowner understand what they have, areas of concern, and what they can do to manage what they have in order to meet their goals for the land. A well-written plan will give the landowner specific projects or jobs to help him or her meet those goals.

For example, a landowner may want to protect water resources but not know what specific steps she can take to do so. A stewardship plan might outline activities such as clearing culverts or making site-specific road repairs to prevent the movement of sediment into a watercourse.

A plan can be very general or detailed, but it should give some background information and touch on major issues of concern. These areas might include roads, soils and erosion, vegetation, fire and fuels reduction, water resources and their protection, wildlife and wildlife habitat, recreation and aesthetics, and special resources such as unstable areas, or archaeological sites.
Even a very basic plan can give a landowner valuable information and guidance. Of course, a plan is only as good as its implementation. But, just as we say a picture is worth a thousand words, a stewardship plan that is followed is worth a thousand good intentions.

Harvesting -- A Middle Way

Every so often a media story passes my desk that looks at whether or not harvests are necessary in order to reduce forest fuels. More often than not, the story addresses clearcuts, and the reporter covers "both sides" by getting quotes from industry and environmental group representatives. Predictably, the two are at polar opposites.

What is usually missing from the to-cut-or-not-to-cut debate, however, is a "middle way "– that is, harvesting options other than clearcuts. There are a lot of silvicultural methods other than clearcuts that are used extensively, and these methods effectively reduce forest fuels.

A prime example is thinning. The purpose of thinning is to reduce the density of trees in the forest, leaving a more vigorous stand that will grow more quickly than if the thinning had not been done. Under the Forest Practice Rules, there are rules that specify how many trees have to be left. For example, on productive forest ground with smaller trees (site class I, II or III with the average tree under 14 inches diameter), 100 trees over 4" diameter per acre must remain after harvest. That's a lot of trees. That's one tree for every circle with a radius of 12 feet. Or if you laid out a square grid, that would be at least one tree every 20 feet. The reality is that more trees than that are left, since people don't want to be penalized for leaving too few trees.

To many people, "harvesting," "clearcut," and "moonscape" are all synonymous. They are not. Not all harvests and clearcuts. Not all clearcuts look like moonscapes, particularly in California. In clearcuts here, the law requires some trees to be left near watercourses and other sensitive areas.

Still, many people believe that all clearcuts are bad and that all harvesting is therefore bad. This is far too a simplistic view and, far from protecting the forests, actually puts them at risk by advocating unrestrained fuels accumulation...until a catastrophic fire comes.

There is a "middle way" in forestry. Both we and the forests will benefit if we can follow it.

Yuba County property owners worked with the US Forest Service to thin their property. The photo on the left shows part of the property where no harvesting was done. The area on the right shows an area that was harvested and underburned (with a low-intensity burn) one year before the photo was taken.

Three Types of Thinning

Imagine a garden in which you've sown carrot seeds. Soon there are dozens of starts coming up, and instinctively you know that you need to pull many of them out so the remaining ones can thrive. In other words, you need to do some thinning.

In the forest, thinning works the same way. When there are too many trees crowding each other, individual trees have less vigor, smaller live crowns, and smaller diameters than their well-spaced cousins.

There are three types of thinning common in forestry. The first, called pre-commercial thinning, is done in stands of trees that are too small to sell commercially. Most trees under about 8" in diameter fall into this category. Since this kind of thinning is expensive to do and doesn't generate any income, it is often left undone. Pre-commercial thinning is most often done in conjunction with a commercial harvest or under a state or federal cost-share program in which the government picks up part of the cost.

Another type of thinning is called commercial thinning. This is done in stands that have a lot of trees per acre of relatively small diameter, at least some of which are merchantable. The goal is to maintain or increase the average stand diameter, removing some trees while leaving healthy, well-spaced trees standing. The "released" trees quickly fill in the spaces created by the thinning and begin to grow bigger (larger diameter).

"Selection" is very similar to commercial thinning. The difference is that it is used in stands with larger diameter trees and fewer trees per acre. Again, the aim is to create a stand with fewer and more well-spaced trees. Healthy, vigorous trees, if they are there to begin with, are often chosen to remain, as they are best able to take full advantage of the new growing space, sunlight and nutrients that become available after the harvest. Most or all of the trees removed under selection are merchantable.

Our forests evolved with periodic fires that thinned them out. Fire suppression coupled with lack of mechanical thinning can lead to disasters like the massive die-off in 2003 of the forests of Lake Arrowhead in southern California. The long-term health of our forests depends on many things, one of which is thinning.

Silvicultural Systems

If you do decide to do active management on your property, how will it look on the ground? Your forester will help you decide what kind of silviculture to use in each area, based on the characteristics of the forest stand but also according to your objectives for the property.

Several silvicultural systems allowed in California are outlined in the Forest Practice Rules. These are divided into "even-aged," "uneven-aged," and "intermediate" systems. Even-aged systems are designed to grow stands of trees that are in the same age class. A stand with an old overstory but a lot of vigorous, well-distributed natural regeneration would be a likely candidate for this kind of system. There is usually just one entry, and the harvest is relatively intense. A "harvestable" tree on most sites is one that is over 60 or 80 years (depending on the site), and younger trees are retained.

Uneven-aged systems maintain at least three distinct age classes of trees. Individual trees or small groups of trees may be harvested under uneven-aged silviculture. Typically this is designed for multiple entries, harvesting relatively little each time. Establishing a new age class can be difficult under this system because existing trees often quickly occupy the "new" growing space made available when individual trees are harvested. Under an NTMP (Non-Industrial Timber Management Plan), uneven-aged silviculture is required.

An example of an "intermediate" system would be a commercial thinning. Depending on how you do the thinning, you could favor developing either an even-aged or uneven-aged stand.

The landowner's objectives – financial, aesthetic, etc. -- are critical in determining the choice of silvicultural system and the intensity of harvest. The more cash a landowner needs, the more likely an intensive harvest will be used. Often the cash the landowner needs to come up with is the cost of the harvest plan, which can easily be over $10,000, and the costs of maintaining the property (taxes, road upkeep, etc.).

As forestry-related regulations become more extensive and intensive, they also become more costly to implement. And the question of who should pay for implementing and enforcing the regulations becomes increasingly important.

Plantation Management

What do you think of when you think of a forest plantation?

The general strategy for managing a plantation is similar the world over. Plantations are managed as even-aged stands, meaning that trees are planted at the same time and, through the life of the stand, are essentially all the same age. The stands may be thinned, but the main harvest happens at the end of the rotation age, when the area is clearcut and regenerated. Plantations help maximize economic return, and by producing a lot of fiber on a small area, can significantly reduce the pressure on forests elsewhere.

But there are important differences in how plantations are managed from region to region. It's not just the species managed that changes, but also basic management addressing issues such as rotation age, level of biodiversity, and planting patterns.

Rotations ages typically vary from less than 10 years to 80 years. Here are some examples – in southeasten China, eucalyptus is managed on 6-year rotations; in the southeast of the US, pine is managed on rotations of 20-25 years; in California, the minimum rotation age is set by law at 50-80 years, depending on the productivity of the site (it is 60 or 80 years for nearly all lands).

The level of biodiversity is linked not only to the tree species present but also the age of the stands. A eucalyptus or acacia monoculture has less diversity than an area planted with a mix of Douglas fir and ponderosa pine. And if those eucalyptus seedlings are grown as clones from cuttings rather than from seed, even within-species (genetic) diversity is lost. As for rotation age, it is fairly intuitive that a forest allowed to grow for 60 years before harvest will develop a stand structure, plant and animal life more complex and diverse than a forest harvested at 6 years.

Planting patterns impact both biodiversity and water quality. Plantations that extend into wet areas or too close to watercourses not only mean loss of the natural riparian vegetation, but also they can put the wet areas and watercourses at risk by increasing water temperature, sedimentation, etc. California has strict requirements set by the state to protect wet areas and watercourses, clearly identifying what resources must be protected and how to do so. Elsewhere, foresters generally decide themselves what to protect and how. Sometimes this works well, but often economic considerations strongly influence decisions, resulting in minimal protection.

There are many other ways in which plantations vary from place to place. The point to remember is that plantations are different the world over, and that plantations in California are some of the best managed in the world.

Cruising and Modeling

There are a number of reasons you might want a "cruise" of your property to determine what kind of timber you have and how much it is worth. A cruise is an important part of an appraisal, used when a property is sold or a conservation easement put in place. The cruise data is also used to help select the best silvicultural system if you choose to actively manage your forest.

Whatever the motivation for having a cruise done, the process is basically the same. A forester begins by obtaining aerial photographs of the project area and drawing boundaries on maps. He or she uses these to stratify the property into "units" based on characteristics such as similar timber type, age class and slope.

The forester then lays out a grid on the map that covers areas of the property to be included in the plan. Walking along that grid, at regular intervals, e.g. every 330 feet, the RPF will stop to gather data on tree density, species, age, height, diameter, health and vigor, rate of growth, spacing, etc.

The data collected during the cruise is entered into a computer and analyzed. The results help the RPF determine what silvicultural system is most appropriate. Because the Forest Practice Rules specify exact standards for trees that may be removed and what must remain after harvest, the data analysis serves to prove that the harvested area will meet those requirements. Key data generally include the number of trees per acre, the "basal area" (horizontal cross-sectional area of the trees at 4.5 feet) per acre, stand age, the species mix before and after harvest, and the quantity, species, and vigor of seedlings and saplings.

For an NTMP, the cruise data is also needed to conduct the Growth and Yield analysis. The cruise data is input into a special forestry modeling program that produces information about current and future harvestable volume, remaining volume, and species composition. The Forest Practice Rules require this analysis to be done for a 100-year period to demonstrate that harvest will not exceed growth in any 10-year interval.

Watershed Assessment

A lot of time, energy and money is being put into the analysis and assessment of watersheds in California. Watershed assessment is about taking an inventory of where you are. It answers the question, What have we got to work with? Watershed analysis addresses what to do with the information gathered in a watershed assessment.

Increasingly, both watershed assessments and analyses are coming under fire for not being extensive and intensive enough. Private landowners and companies currently shoulder a significant share of these costs in terms of doing surveys and assessments that are required for land management activities (like harvesting timber). Over the next few years, it is very likely that additional dollars will be contributed by various state and federal government agencies to expand these assessment efforts.

Watershed assessment is no simple task, and it can encompass many different areas. One assessment might focus on existing roads, trying to find answers to questions like: How much sediment do they deliver to watercourse? How much sediment are which roads likely to deliver in the future? Can some of the roads be decommissioned and, if so, which ones? Another assessment might focus on streams, collecting data on stream temperature, sediment loads, gravel embeddedness, woody debris availability, etc. Still another assessment might focus on the types and conditions of various habitat types, including information like fuel loading or the availability of snags or downed woody debris.

Another question is the level of depth of an analysis. Some analysis can be done in the office. Road densities or stand types, for examples, might be estimated from aerial photos. But many analyses require direct measurements in the field. And while some measurements can be made by electronic devises, ultimately a person is needed to monitor those devices and collect the information.

There are seemingly endless other questions such as: How large a geographic area should you consider? How long do you monitor? How do you know when you no longer need to collect data? Can data collection or monitoring be reduced to a few key indicators? If so, what are those indicators?

The fact is that we simply don't have the financial and personnel resources to do complete assessment on all our watersheds. We live in the real world where time and money are limited, and we need to prioritize what information is most valuable. And we need to remember that while some of this information may be most efficiently collected by government resource specialists, other information will need to come from on-the-ground resource managers.

Watershed Analysis

What is done with the data collected in a watershed assessment? It is used to help determine what to do next in terms of resource management. In other words, it is used to begin the watershed analysis. The analysis answers the question, What should we do with the resources?

The key role of local land managers in the analysis and use of watershed assessment information cannot be overemphasized. These local professionals are in a unique position to be able to interpret the general assessment. Since we don't have the time and money to assess every resource in every watershed, we need to rely on local land managers who can look at data from the broader assessment and pinpoint what additional data is needed and from where.

In other words, the local professionals should be allowed the freedom to use professional judgment in analyzing, interpreting, and using the data. Over the past decade, the ability of our land managers to exercise professional judgment has been severely eroded. The push at the state level for more extensive and intensive watershed assessment and analysis done at the state level (not by local resource professionals) threatens to remove from local land managers even more decision-making ability.

There are roles for the state to play in watershed analysis. The presentation and dissemination of information is one example. The internet offers tremendous possibilities—imagine a website where you could click on Mendocino County and access data on the Eel River, or look at a map that shows relative risk of catastrophic fire in El Dorado County. CD-ROMs offer another way to get information out cheaply to folks who need it.

Of course we need to ensure that our watersheds remain healthy and productive. The way to accomplish this is by focusing on desired end results and taking advantage of the years of experience of local land managers, working together to achieve those results. What we need to avoid is devolving even deeper into the morass of numerous and detailed restrictions and prescriptions that are blanketly applied across the state and that are often based on politics rather than science.

Part III -- Sustaining California's Forests

Keepers of the Forest – California's Forest Landowners

One Family's Forest

In Santa Cruz County I had the opportunity to visit a wonderful family-owned redwood forest. Though the forest has been logged twice in the last 15 years, unless you looked for the stumps on the ground, you'd never know it. The forester who manages the property said that he had a visit from a woman who was concerned about logging. She looked around and asked when the forest they were looking at would be logged. In fact they were standing in the middle of an area in which logging had just been completed.

When most people think of logging, they have in mind the image of a clearcut. What they don't think about are the kinds of logging that leave a lot of trees standing. The kind of silviculture that was used in the redwood forest I visited was "selection," which is essentially thinning. The strategy of the foresters is to go in every 12-15 years and harvest about 1/3 of the volume. Even with these harvests, the forest grows more than is cut. So, for example, if they have 6 million board feet in 2002 and harvest 2 million, by the time they go in again in 2014, the forest will once again have more than 6 million board feet.

In other words, the harvest is sustainable. The foresters have been using this strategy for over 30 years, and they now have a healthy forest that produces some of the best redwood timber around. It also has some of the best recreation opportunities and habitat for fish and wildlife in the area.

The owners enjoy the property, which has been in the family for generations. They recognize its value for wildlife, water, aesthetics, and recreation. Their forest is home to threatened and endangered species for which the foresters set aside habitat. Some people think the management of the property is so good that they are lobbying to get the local parks to adopt a similar style of management.

This family's forest is in an area threatened by development. The forest is about the same size of the nearest city, where housing is scarce and land prices are sky-high. If the owners were only looking at the economics, they would sell out, subdividing the forest into parcels for residential development. Doing so would degrade wildlife habitat, water quality, and the aesthetics of

the area. We need to recognize families like this whose efforts, and whose financial sacrifices, benefit our forests, our wildlife, and ourselves.

*This photo was taken just **after** selection logging in this redwood forest had been completed. The family chooses to keep this area as a working forest but could make a fortune by creating a residential subdivision.*

Analysis Paralysis

At a forestry professional society meeting in 2002, the USFS Regional Forester for California Jack Blackwell spoke at length about the problem of "analysis paralysis" in the Forest Service. The Forest Service had just released a report called "The Process Predicament," reiterating Blackwell's assessment that the Forest Service is mired in red tape.

The report (available at www.fs.fed.us) indicates that planning and assessment eats up as much as $250 million each year, or 40% of the "direct work at the national forest level." An internal Forest Service estimate says that "inefficiencies" consume at least $100 million at the project level.

But it's not just the Forest Service that is bogged down in red tape. Ask any forest landowner who has had a harvest plan written in the last few years and you'll get an earful of the red tape private landowners and their foresters go through to get a harvesting permit in California. An informal survey I did in 2002 indicated that the estimated cost for a typical 160-acre harvest plan in Mendocino County was about $20,000. This only covers getting the permit and does not include the costs of logging, log hauling, timber yield taxes, or work on roads.

The point is that laws and regulations, as well as the cost of implementing them, should be workable in the real world. They shouldn't prevent needed work from being done in a timely way. Whether it's salvage logging on a national forest to reduce fire risk, or a landowner trying to harvest a few trees to pay the expenses that are all part of good and responsible forest stewardship, the laws and regulations should encourage and even reward this work. They shouldn't result in "analysis paralysis" that results in nothing being done.

Trying to Do The Right Thing

In the Cherry Creek subdivision north of Willits, I walked the property of a forest landowner who wants to "do the right thing." He is not particularly interested in logging, and he is willing to spend some money out of pocket to improve his piece of the forest. He is not a poor man, but he is not a rich man, either. The dollars he has to spend are limited.

There is a lot of work he could do. He could focus his time and energy on the roads to reduce erosion. He could put a culvert in the old washed-out crossing that is actively eroding. He could rock the edge of drainage structures in the road so they don't continue to erode the edges of the road. He could dig ditches to drain the water that occasionally cuts small gullies in the road surface.

Or he could focus his efforts on improving the health of the trees. He could do this by thinning out the pockets of doghair thickets of both conifer and hardwood regeneration. Or he could cut the old, suppressed understory conifers that will never become much bigger than they are, giving more sunlight, water and nutrients to the younger trees with the goal of growing a few, very large trees like what the stumps on the ground suggest existed years ago.

Doghair thickets like this one of Douglas-fir are not uncommon in our forests in which fire has been excluded.

The reality of it is that most of this work never will be done. What will likely be done is some thinning to protect the house against catastrophic wildfire. If the landowner is ambitious, he may expand the scope of this work to 50 or 100 feet on either side of the road along the ridge, which will help contain any fire. He may or may not do the roadwork, which is located in areas of the property he rarely visits. And he will still be able to access by ATV or by foot for several years, until a bad winter washes out portions of the road completely.

The fact that most of the needed work will probably not be done is through no fault of the landowner. He is doing everything he can, given his limited resources. The dollars from the state to help pay for these kinds of activity have shrunk to virtually nothing with the suspension of logging from Jackson State Forest. And even if the landowner wanted to harvest timber and reinvest the money in the land, I would advise him against it, at least under our current regulatory environment. The plan would be so costly and his timber volume per acre so low that his only hope of breaking even would be harvest his lands so heavily that he would not like the end result.

How ironic that the landowner who most wants to do the right thing for his land finds it so difficult to do so.

High Plan Costs for Forest Landowners

Landowners interested in harvesting timber have been experiencing sticker shock for quite a few years, and it is getting worse. Despite the fact that various state and federal agencies recognize that there is a problem and have met in Sacramento to try to hammer out some kind of relief for small landowners, the price of managing timber continues to rise.

Plan costs for Timber Harvest Plans in California are staggering. A landowner with one or two hundred acres in Mendocino or Humboldt County typically pays in the neighborhood of $15,000 - $25,000 for a harvesting plan (in 2002), and sometimes more. On top of that are costs for logging, hauling, road work, taxes, and fees. Depending on when the plan is begun, the process can take six months to a year or more. That is a long time to tie up what for most of us is the better part of a year's salary.

While landowners may have a lot of value in their property, most don't have a lot of cash. The end result is that many landowners simply can't afford to manage their property. For those who think that's a good thing, it's important to remember that inactive land management comes with its own challenges and concerns. A few of these include importing more wood from places with less strict environmental regulations than we have here, the buildup of fuels, continued bleeding of sediment from old poorly-constructed roads and crossings, and fewer tax dollars being generated.

Those who do manage to pay for harvesting plans have huge plan costs that need to be recovered. You have to cut a lot of trees just to break even for a $20,000 plan, not to mention the additional costs.

Extremely high plan costs, intense regulation, low timber prices, and development pressures make the alternative of subdividing a property and selling off parcels increasingly attractive. As increasing numbers of homes dot the landscape and year-round residents build roads to their homesites, we will see the risk of catastrophic wildfire rise while our forests become more fragmented.

The Landowner and Surveying for Murrelets

On the Sonoma County coast, I spent the day with a forester who works on properties where marbled murrelets sometimes occur. The marbled murrelet is of course a protected species, and for a forester that means extra steps to be taken in preparing a harvest plan. This particular forester, who is an excellent steward of the land, agrees that murrelets should be protected. But, as he points out, there are two real hardships for landowners in how things are done right now.

First, the state agency that has to determine whether or not there is potential habitat is apparently overworked and understaffed, and the agency can go for months at a time without making a decision. The forester recently waited four months for a decision, which finally came after the logging season was over. The landowner had many thousands of dollars invested in the plan, and the 4-month delay meant that logging couldn't start until well into the next year. Not many of us would be willing to tie up $10,000-$20,000 for nearly a year without any compensation, but that is exactly what happened to this landowner.

Second, in addition to tying up funds, the landowner bears the entire cost of the survey itself. And it is expensive. For every 40 acres that have to be included in the survey, the cost to the landowner this forester works with is about $2,000. If the landowner is cash-poor, as many are, that means that more trees will be cut to pay for the surveys.

The forester on the Sonoma coast explained that the log prices he could get for his client were very low, particularly for fir. Based on the prices he could get, the landowner would get about $150 for a redwood 15 inches in diameter and 100 feet tall (about 250 board feet in volume), or $65 for a Douglas-fir of the same size. At those prices, he would have to cut 13 redwoods or 31 Douglas-firs just to cover the cost of a murrelet survey for 40 acres. It's simply more than a lot of landowners are willing to do.

The result is more and more landowners doing nothing, neglecting all management of forests, roads, and wildlife habitat. At the same time, conversion to non-forest uses becomes an increasingly attractive alternative. Once again, this is a case of the best of intentions leading to unintended negative consequences for both forest landowners and their forests.

Planting -- Order Seedlings in the Fall

Fall is the time to start planning your fall and winter planting and to order seedlings, even if you don't want your seedlings for several months. The sooner you get your order in, the better the chances of getting the seedlings of your choice (species, age, container vs. bareroot) and seedlings from your seed zone. The CDF nurseries are good seedling sources and usually start taking orders in early November.

Costs for bareroot seedlings in 2002 were around $265 per thousand for two-year-old conifers or one-year-old hardwoods. Costs for container seedlings are higher, at about $500 for 1,000 conifers and $565 for 1,000 hardwoods in 2002. Smaller quantities are available, but plan on buying seedlings in minimum quantities of 100 for bareroot or 50 for containers.

You can order your seedlings early and specify when you want them delivered. You can also pick them up yourself, but most people opt for UPS delivery. Shipments can be made anytime before May 1, except for container redwoods, which need to go out before February 1.

No matter where you are in the state, you can buy seedlings from the CDF nursery. They grow seedlings from seed zones based on location and elevation all over California. The nursery staff is very knowledgeable and can answer your questions about what kind of seedlings are right for you and how to take care of them. If you have questions or would like to get a price list and order form, call them at 530-873-0400 or 530-753-2441. They also have a website at http://calfire.ca.gov/resource_mgt/resource_mgt_statenurseries.php. If you would rather buy from a private nursery, check the Yellow Pages or call the Forestry Helpline (800-738-8733) for information on nurseries in your area.

Planting – Bareroot or Container Seedlings?

For folks who have forest in areas with rainy rather than snowy winters, holiday time is usually when it is getting to be that time of year again—time to plant seedlings. A variety of hardwood and softwood seedlings is available from nurseries. One of the most common questions is whether to buy bareroot or container stock.

Container seedlings are grown and shipped in small plastic containers. These usually hold a little more than 12 cubic inches of soil. The tree planter removes the container just before planting the tree, so the tree is actually planted with the soil it was grown in.

Bareroot seedlings, by contrast, are pulled up at the nursery and shipped without a significant amount of soil. The key to protecting your bareroot seedlings is to keep them cool and minimize the exposure of their roots to the air.

Seedlings should be stored at a temperature of less than 40 degrees. Nursery staff at the CDF nursery in Magalia suggest that if proper refrigeration is not available, keep your seedlings cool using a "poor man's icebox" – a block of ice and some plastic bags.

Remember that seed zone is very important when ordering your seedlings. The seed zone is based on the latitude, longitude, and elevation of your property. If you have this information (a legal description and elevational range will do), the folks at the CDF nursery will be able to help you determine what your seed zone is.

To check on availability of bareroot stock, call the Magalia Reforestation Center at 530-873-0400. For container seedlings, call the L.A. Moran Reforestation Center in Davis at 530-753-2441. Both are operated by CDF staff who can not only check on availability but also can answer questions about your planting project.

Pruning for Aesthetics and Fire Safety

Have you thought about pruning your trees? There are two good reasons to do so. In addition to improving visual aesthetics by opening up the view, pruning also decreases fire risk.

The winter is a particularly good time to prune. This is because winter is the dormant season, and by pruning in the cold weather, you'll have less sap flow. Winter is also the time when beetles are most inactive.

One of the immediate benefits of pruning is that you can open up your view. Whether you want to see farther into the forest or better enjoy a long-distance mountain view, pruning lower branches will allow your eye to see farther.

In addition, pruning helps produce higher-quality wood, as it reduces the number of knots. In places like New Zealand, forest managers spend a lot of time and money pruning in order to get the highest-quality logs they can.

But perhaps the most important advantage of pruning is to reduce your risk of fire. Low-hanging limbs are one kind of "fuel ladder" that makes it easier for flames to climb from the forest floor into the crowns of trees. By increasing the height of the lowest branches, it becomes more difficult for flames to reach the needles, leaves, and twigs that can ignite so easily.

How high up should you prune? For small trees, leave 40% or more of the total tree height in "live crown" (not pruned). For tall trees, prune as high as you can safely, usually 8 to 15 feet. You can prune higher limbs with a pole saw (a curved saw on an extension pole). Be sure to make an undercut for larger limbs so that when the branch falls it doesn't strip off bark from the bole of the tree. It's a great workout for your upper arms!

Pruning and Burning Snow Breakage

The winter months sometimes bring heavy snow that breaks the branches of trees and shrubs. On steep slopes, some trees and shrubs can simply gave way and be uprooted. In other areas, tree tops or large branches may break off and block roads.

When you break out your chainsaw to clear the branches and shrubs from the road or elsewhere, here are a few things to keep in mind.

> If you have trees or shrubs on a slope, such as the cutbank adjacent to a road, that are uprooted and need to be removed, consider establishing new vegetation. This will help maintain the stability of the slope. You can buy your shrubs, or you can take small nearby shrubs or trees and simply transplant them.

> Help damaged trees heal their wounds by pruning limbs that were broken by the snow. Don't cut flush against the tree trunk, as you will cut into the "branch collar" (a raised area where the branch and the trunk come together) that contains chemicals that inhibit the spread of decay. Information on pruning technique is available at the Forest Steward website, at http://ceres.ca.gov/foreststeward/prune.html. Or call 800-738-8733 (e-mail ncsaf@mcn.org) and ask for a copy of the winter 1999 Forestland Steward Newsletter article on pruning.

> You can scatter the vegetation you cut along the forest floor or create piles to burn later.

> If you make piles, keep them under 4 feet in diameter and burn them before April 30. If you have more material, make a second pile and feed material from it into the 4-foot pile when you are burning. If your pile is over 4 feet in diameter, things get more complicated. And after the first of May, you'll need an additional permit from CDF and may have to have the pile inspected. So keep your pile small and burn it soon.

Put organic material like limbs, leaves, and pine needles into the pile, but keep out clods of dirt. This will help the pile burn more cleanly when you do burn it.

On the day you plan to burn your pile, call Air Quality to make sure it is a "permissive burn day." The number is 800-392-6278.

If you have any questions about your pile or burning, call your local Fire Department.

Recovering from Fire--Logging

What is a forest landowner with the burned-over land to do once the smoke clears?

In many areas, many trees left after a fire will be dead or dying and yet will still have merchantable wood. In addition to generating some cash, removing the merchantable logs will reduce the amount fuel available for future wildfires.

As you know, in California, if you want to harvest any wood for commercial purposes, you have to have a permit from the California Department of Forestry. That includes harvesting of fire-killed or fire-damaged trees.

To address such conditions, there is a special kind of permit called an "Emergency Notice" that can be used to harvest timber. Trees that can be harvested include those "that are fallen, damaged, dead or dying as a result of wind, snow, freezing weather, fire, flood, landslide or earthquake." (A "dying" tree is one has more than half its foliage turn brown or that will, in the professional judgment of the RPF, likely die within one year.)

The Emergency Notice has to be prepared by a Registered Professional Forester, who must substantiate that emergency conditions exist. This kind of Notice is simpler and faster to get through the system than a regular Timber Harvest Plan. Because the Emergency Notice is designed to respond to emergency conditions, it assumes that a landowner will get to work right away, and the Notice is only valid for 120 days.

Insects and fungi quickly attack burned timber, so a landowner who believes she has merchantable logs left after a fire should not delay in contacting a forester.

Recovering from Fire--Planting

Whether or not you salvage merchantable timber from your property after a fire, it's important to plant trees to re-establish the forest.

Brush, grass and hardwood species all re-establish themselves quickly after a fire. Many grow much more quickly than conifers in the first few years. A delay in planting will allow those "competing" species to occupy most if not all of the growing space. While a few conifers will re-establish themselves (if the site is suitable for conifers), there will be intense competition for sunlight, water and nutrients. There will be relatively few conifers, and they will grow slowly. While surviving mature conifers can be a good source of seed, planted seedlings that are already a year or two old will have a significant competitive advantage over the other vegetation. And you'll still end up with plenty of brush, grass and hardwoods.

Your hardwood species will grow stump-sprouts after a fire. Consider thinning the sprouts in the first years after the burn. This will give you fewer, larger stems. Larger stems will be of higher value than smaller stems, whether you intend to use them as logs, firewood, or for wildlife habitat.

Depending on the specifics of your situation, you may qualify for financial assistance with planting under the CFIP (California Forest Improvement Program) or other cost share programs. Call the Forestry Helpline (800-738-8733) for the name and number of your local CDF service forester to contact for more information.

Thinning

The long days of summer can be a good time to do thinning of small trees on your property. Many areas in our state are in dire need of "pre-commercial thinning," or thinning of stems that are such small diameter that they don't have economic value. Other areas can benefit from thinning of trees that do have commercial value. Historically, fires thinned trees of various sizes our forest stands. Now that we suppress fire, we have a high number of trees per acre and have many areas with too many trees.

How do you decide which trees to cut and which trees to keep? First of all, look at the health and vigor of the trees. Ideally, you want to keep trees that have good "live crown ratios," or the percentage of the tree, from the ground to the very top, that has live needles. For conifers, you want trees with a 30-40% live crown ratio (more is OK but hard to find in a stand that needs to be thinned). In dense stands, your trees may have less than 30% live crown, so leave the ones that have the highest live crown ratio.

Another important consideration is spacing. You might use the "DBH+4" rule-of-thumb. Estimate or measure the diameter of the tree in inches. Convert it to feet and add four to get your recommended spacing between trees. So for a 6-inch DBH tree, you'd want the nearest tree in any direction to be no closer than 10 feet.

Pre-commercial thinning does not have to be done under a THP, since you aren't selling what you cut. But remember that if you do cut any wood for sale, trade, or barter, you must have an approved Timber Harvest Plan (THP) or other state-approved plan.

Portions of the 40-year old Ponderosa pine stand in the Tahoe National Forest were thinned as part of the Forest Divide Project to protect local communities. On the left is an unthinned area. On the right is a thinned area that was also underburned.

Thinning and Crown Classification

While live crown ratios and spacing between trees may well be the most important factors in helping you decide which trees to keep and which trees to thin, another factor you might consider is crown classification.

There are four crown classifications: dominant, co-dominant, intermediate, and suppressed. The crown, or green branches, of a dominant tree gets a lot of sunlight from above and quite a bit from the sides. Co-dominant trees also receive light from above but not very much from the sides. Intermediate trees are shorter than dominants and co-dominants. Their crowns are usually small but have managed to grow up into the crown layer of the dominants and co-dominants. Suppressed trees have small crowns which are completely below the crown layer of the other three classes. Intermediates and suppressed trees receive little or no direct sunlight.

When thinning, you generally want to leave your dominant and co-dominant trees. When you thin, you increase the amount of sunlight, water and nutrients available to your "leave trees." The dominants and co-dominants, typically the biggest and most vigorous trees in your forest, will be best able to take immediate advantage of these increased resources.

An excellent resource on thinning is a little pamphlet called "Thinning," which is put out by the University of California Cooperative Extension. It covers topics such as basic tree growth, how thinning effects growth of individuals trees as well as the forest stand, when to thin, and how to thin. If you are planning on thinning your property, call the Forest Stewardship Helpline (1-800-738-TREE) for a copy of this wonderful 10-page resource.

Roads -- Winterizing Them

When the rains of winter come, it is a reminder that if you haven't already done so, it's time to "winterize" your roads. Here are some things to do:

Culverts: Make sure the inlets and outlets are free of debris and accumulated sediment. If you have trash racks, clear the debris away from them.

Ditches: Clear out debris and soil so that the ditch will be able to handle the flow of water. You may want to remove weeds, but don't take out more than you really need to, as the vegetation can act as a useful sediment filter.

Waterbars: Make sure that these are in place. If people have been driving over existing waterbars, you may need to repair them so that they will drain the water off the road.

Rolling dips: Check the "lip" of the dip, where the water drains off the road. If it looks like the road surface at the lip has been eroded, you might want to reinforce it with rocks or bags of cement to prevent further erosion.

Gates: If you have trouble keeping vehicles off a road, keep it gated. A "gate" as simple as a cable stretched between two trees can help keep unwelcome vehicles off your road.

Particularly if you have new roads, it is important to walk them during or just after a big storm. And whether your road is old or new, you will want to constantly keep an eye on your culverts to make sure they have not gotten partially plugged. The goal is to spot drainage problems while they are still small and can be fixed relatively easily.

Roads -- Clean Your Culverts

By cleaning out your culverts, you will be helping ensure that storm runoff will be able to flow freely through the culvert, allowing it to function as it was designed. Otherwise, water may accumulate around the inlet, causing erosion of the fill. In serious cases, this can weaken the fill to the point the culvert blows out entirely. It's much simpler to take some time to maintain the crossings before a problem arises.

If you know exactly where your culverts are, you can drive right to each one. If you are new to the property or just aren't quite sure where your culverts are, take a shovel and walk the roads. Walk down to the inlet and outlet and clean out any large debris that has accumulated. If there are a few small pieces of debris, like leaves and twigs, that look like they will flow freely when the rains come, you can leave those. But be sure to move large accumulations of small materials, as well as larger branches or rocks that have fallen down and will block the flow of water. Also look down through the culvert to make sure there aren't big rocks or branches inside the culvert itself. If there are, you'll want to move them out.

For smaller culverts (under about 18 inches in diameter), you may find that leaves and twigs cover most or all of the inlet. Move the material to where it won't be carried back down to the culvert inlet. Some small-diameter culvert inlets become hidden pretty easily, so you might carry some kind of marker, such as fence posts or paint, to mark any hard-to-see culverts so you can find them easily in the future.

It's important to note that if large branches or rocks are helping stabilize the soil around the inlet or outlet, you'll probably want to leave them in place. It's the ones that aren't stabilizing the soil and will block the free flow of water that you want to clear out.

Clean out your culverts every year. If you have difficulty finding your culverts, use fence posts or other markers to note the culverts' locations.

Cleaning your culverts is a simple process, although if you have a lot of culverts on your property, it can be time-consuming. But doing proper maintenance will save you a lot of headaches and dollars down the road.

How to Find a Forester

If you know what a Registered Professional Forester (RPF) is and think that you need one, how do you find one?

Local resources include the local California Department of Forestry office, which maintains a local list of RPFs that is available to the public. Another resource is sawmills, which often have staff foresters. These foresters may be available to come look at your woods and recommend an RPF who may or may not work for the mill. You can also refer to ads in the Yellow Pages (under "Foresters--consulting").

At the state level, there are two resources for finding foresters. One is Professional Foresters Registration, who does the actual licensing of foresters. For $3.00 they will send you a list of the RPFs in the state who have requested that their names be included in such inquiries.

A smaller statewide list is maintained by the Association of Consulting Foresters and is available on the internet at http://www.acf-foresters.org/Content/NavigationMenu/FindaForester/MapaForester/default.htm. While this site lists only about 25 foresters for the entire state, it also includes many e-mail and website links to RPFs. You can also try various internet search engines using key words such as "consulting forester" and the county name.

Finally, there is the tried and true method of word-of-mouth. Ask your neighboring landowners if they have worked with a forester they have liked. Before hiring him or her for a job, meet with the forester to make sure you can communicate clearly with each other. If you don't know other landowners who can recommend a forester, keep an eye open for announcements for workshops put on by groups such as the Forest Landowners of California, Institute for Sustainable Forestry or your local Resource Conservation District, as often these events attract quite a few forest landowners. Refer to the Natural Resources Electronic Calendar at http://danr.ucop.edu/ihrmp/nrn.html, or call the Forestry Helpline at 800-738-8733 for dates and locations of workshops.

The Pest Detection Form

There's new life for an old form -- the Forest Pest Detection Report. This form has been around for a long time, but many people are not very familiar with it or haven't known how to access it. So the California Department of Forestry decided in 2002 to post the form on its website in hopes that forest landowners, resource managers, and others will make use of it.

You can use the form to report any forest pest that is affecting any part of the tree –foliage, buds, cones, the leader, twigs, branches, the bole, or roots. Pests you can report include insects, diseases, animals, weeds, in addition to damage caused by chemicals, machines, or weather.

The purpose of the form is twofold. The first is to help identify and document the scope of damage from forest pests. Information gathered from individuals who send in the forms is compiled and published in an annual report titled Forest Pest Conditions.

The second purpose of the form is to help people identify the forest pest they have spotted. When you send in the form, you can attach a sample to be identified. As a private individual, you send the form and the sample (if you have one) to a CDF office. The form includes addresses for three CDF Forest Pest Management offices throughout the state. If you are a zone of infestation for Sudden Oak Death, contact the Forest Pest Management Office before sending in any sample you think might be Sudden Oak Death.

The Forest Detection Report form is part of a cooperative project that is sponsored by the California Forest Pest Council. Partners include the US Forest Service and CDF. You can download the form from the CDF website at www.fire.ca.gov/resource_mgt/downloads/fpdrfill.doc. To view a copy of the annual report "Forest Pest Conditions," visit http://www.fs.usda.gov/detail/r5/forest-grasslandhealth/?cid=fsbdev3_046704.

Roads – Why and How to Manage Them

Roads and Sediment

Roads are widely recognized as the single biggest source of sediment to our watercourses. That's important to remember when making decisions about using, repairing, or building roads.

Sediment carried by flowing water is oblivious to the use the road was designed for. Regardless of whether road is used for home access, recreation, forestry, or fire fighting, if it is poorly constructed or not properly maintained, it will be a source of sediment that will be carried into watercourses.

There are a few things we can do to reduce the amount of sediment transported from roads into watercourses.

First, minimize travel on dirt roads during rainy or very wet periods. If you do have to travel on a dirt road regularly year-round, consider putting rock on the road where it runs along a watercourse or any place it looks like road runoff would make it to a watercourse. The rock will help stabilize things and reduce the movement of sediment.

Second, minimize the construction of new roads. If you do need to put in a new road, spend the money to hire someone who can design it properly. A lot of dirt gets moved around when a new road is put in, and if it isn't well designed, there is a risk of altering drainage patterns and significantly increasing erosion.

This gully was formed by poor drainage from a road put in place to access new homes. It continues to "bleed" sediment every year.

Third, when reconstructing or maintaining an existing road, always work to minimize the potential for erosion. This means outsloping rather than insloping (in most cases), using rolling dips instead of culverts where possible, cleaning out culverts regularly, etc. If you're not sure exactly what to do, get the **Handbook for Forest and Ranch Roads** from the Mendocino County Resource Conservation District and use it as your reference guide.

Proper maintenance of roads is an important part of forest stewardship, whether you have half an acre or a hundred acres. What you do or don't do makes a difference.

Learning About Roads

A forest landowner and I were talking about how far a little bit of knowledge can go in terms of road maintenance. He has made sure that on his 80 acres the roads are low-maintenance and kept in good condition. That's a good course of action for any landowner.

It's in the best interest of landowners, forests, and fish to learn about how to build and maintain roads. Even if you hire someone else to do road work, having some basic knowledge and making clear to the equipment operator what you want (and what you want to avoid) can mean the difference between having a road that will need maintenance and repairs on a regular basis and having one that will be virtually worry-free, low-maintenance, and that keeps sediment out of the watercourses.

Each spring, equipment is fired up to work on existing roads and put in new ones. But before putting a cat blade down or getting the grader out, it's a good idea to take some time to learn about things like outsloping, rolling dips, and "fail-safe" culvert design. Occasionally local workshops are sponsored by organizations like UC Cooperative Extension, Resource Conservation Districts (RCDs), or local watershed councils. Usually one-day workshops, these are an excellent investment of your time.

In terms of written references, one of the best roads books for landowners and foresters I've ever come across is the ***Handbook for Forest and Ranch Roads***, printed by the Mendocino County RCD. This user-friendly and practical book describes the basics of roads and provides some pictures of what can happen if a road isn't built or maintained properly. With diagrams, readable text, and many pictures, this book is an excellent resource. Copies are available from the RCD at 707-468-9223, extension 3, or at 405 S. Orchard in Ukiah, CA 95482.

Another option is to have a professional forester or other natural resource professional review your road plan. Whether your plan is simply some ideas you have or something more formal that's written down, having the advice of a professional can help tremendously.

Regardless of where you get your advice or information, the point is to do so before work begins. This is one ounce of prevention that can pay big dividends by preventing many pounds of costly cure.

Invisible Roads

You have probably never thought about your road being invisible, but it's something you should consider. Invisible to flowing water, that is.

Roads are recognized as the single biggest source of sediment into watercourses. And sediment can travel as easily from a ranch road or access road to a summer cabin as from a logging road. The goal for all of these roads is to reduce the sediment transported as much as possible.

The best way to do this is to make the roads "hydrologically invisible." That's a fancy term that means the water flows down the hill in the same places as it did before the road was put in. In other words, you want your road to not make any difference in how the water flows.

One thing you can do is to avoid long ditches where water is channeled for a long way. The water builds up speed and quantity as it flows. The farther and faster it goes, the greater its ability to erode. The goal is to get the water off and across the road as quickly as possible.

Often you will have water that builds up on the surface of the road, creating little gullies. These gullies can erode the surface of the road and transport sediment. The fix is to put in a little dip or a little water bar that will catch the water and channel it off the road, preferably into some vegetation that can slow the flow of the water and trap any sediment.

Do your best to make your road hydrologically "invisible." Not only will it benefit your watercourses, but it may well reduce long-term road maintenance costs as well.

Summer Road Work and Winter Rains

A landowner who has done a lot of work constructing footpaths on his property was talking about the paths that he has constructed that give him access to his beloved forest. They are well made and stable, he said, before adding as an afterthought that he does have to do quite a bit of repair work each year after the rains. That indicates the paths aren't as stable as he thinks.

Winter rains are one of the real tests of how well a path or a road was constructed. A stable road or path is one that can withstand those winter rains without needing a lot of repairs and that, as a by-product of that stability, has minimal movement of soil into watercourses.

One crucial step in constructing stable trails or roads is to know where the small watercourses are. That's not as easy as it sounds, because many watercourses are dry for most of the year. In fact, there can be watercourses that have a "channel" the size of your cupped hand that might only run water a few days in typical years. In dry years, they might not run any water at all. But in years with heavy rainfall, these small watercourses can damage your road or trail and wash sediment downstream.

When you determine where the watercourses are, a relatively quick and easy way to protect the soil is to first make sure the "channel" is far enough below the road grade or trail grade so that water will run across, and not down, the road or trail. Next, put down rock (or bags of cement) over the area where the water will flow, making sure that the "crossing" that you are creating is still low enough to ensure that the water will flow across.

There are two important things to remember. First, put down big enough pieces of rock that the flowing water won't wash them away. The bigger the estimated flow, the bigger the rocks you will need. Second, it's especially important to "armor" the outside edge, where the water actually drops off the road or trail surface.

Because a lot of road and trail work is done in the summer, it can be easy to miss watercourses or to seriously underestimate how much water will flow in them come winter. The best test is to walk your roads or trails in the winter, preferably during a good storm, armed with your favorite hand tool and ready to make a few repairs.

These landowners found that a culvert on their road had plugged during a storm. Water flowed over the road surface until they were able to clear the inlet.

Watercourse Crossings -- "And This Too Will Change"

"'And this too will change' -- the universal truth for watersheds and everything else." This was the opening remark of a geologist at a conference on watercourse crossings. He made this comment to remind us that when replacing or putting in new watercourse crossings, it's important to take a very long-term view, stepping back to look at the big picture and to ask some basic questions.

First, is the crossing really needed? Good planning can minimize the number of crossings. For example, if people are putting in houses on one side of a watercourse, it makes more sense to construct a road that crosses the watercourse once, instead of having a separate crossing for each house. The principle here is the fewer, the better, since many crossings eventually fail.

Second, is the kind of crossing being well chosen and designed? A poorly chosen or poorly designed crossing will fail sooner. For example, the best crossing for an ephemeral stream is often not a culvert but a rolling dip or a dry ford with large rock. When a culvert is needed, it should be large enough to carry not only water but also debris that the water will likely be carrying.

Third, what will happen when the crossing fails? This is particularly important for culverts. If the culvert plugs and blows out, is the crossing designed so that the water will stay in the existing channel? Or will it run down the road, cutting a new channel and carrying massive amounts of sediment with it?

Finally, is there a plan to maintain the crossings? Culverts in particular, but also other kinds of crossings, need regular monitoring and maintenance. That gives the landowner a chance to catch small problems before they become big problems.

There's no question that we need crossings. We need them to get to our homes, jobsites, restoration sites, fire trails, and campgrounds. Our goal should be to make sure those crossings are designed well and with the understanding that they are part of a dynamic landscape that changes over time.

Low-Maintenance Stream Crossings

Summer is a good time to start those roads projects you have had in mind. If that includes repairing or putting in stream crossings, consider whether or not a low-maintenance crossing is appropriate for you.

Culverts make fore high-maintenance crossings. You need to inspect the inlets and outlets every year, clearing away branches and debris, both before the rainy season begins and also after big storms. Culverts eventually need to be replaced, which means buying a new pipe, digging out and disposing of the old one, and installing the new one. All in all, it's a lot of work to maintain a culvert that functions properly.

A lower-maintenance alternative is the rolling dip. Rolling dips are depressions in the road grade that roll down and back up again, forming a dip that you can drive over slowly. These work very well for small watercourses on road grades that are not too steep.

For larger watercourses, rocked fords are sometimes used. On these crossings, you actually drive over the streambed. It's important to have good

A rolling dip is a depression in the road grade deep enough to allow for the passage of water over the road surface but shallow enough that you can drive over it.

gravel or rocks so that they won't be pulverized by the weight of the passing vehicles, and also to do any work on the ford when the crossing is dry or when water flows are lowest. It's a good idea to inspect fords periodically and to add rock as needed.

Rolling dips and fords are appropriate for many, but not all, crossings where culverts have traditionally been used. These crossings will mean lower maintenance for you in terms of both time and dollars over the years. For more information on rolling dips, rocked fords, and other crossings, read the ***Handbook for Forest and Ranch Roads***.

Rolling dips

Rolling dips are frequently used for small watercourses, the kind that run intermittently. A stream that runs water **any** time of the year is a candidate for a rolling dip. Rolling dips are also used to prevent road surface erosion by draining water that collects and starts to channel along the surface of the road.

Rolling dips are essentially depressions in the road grade. They get their name from the grade of the road "rolling" down and back up again, thus forming the dip. In the case of a small watercourse, the water flows directly across the road over the lowest point of the dip. In the case of road surface runoff, the water running down the middle of the road is caught in the dip and drained to the side.

Rolling dips are, relative to waterbars, much easier to drive over and are not damaged by vehicle traffic. If properly constructed, they require virtually no maintenance. That is of particular value to a non-resident landowner or one who is often away from the property in the winter.

A common problem with rolling dips is that where the water runs off the road, it can erode the edge of the road surface. The solution is to armor that edge, or "lip," with materials that won't erode, such as rock or bags of cement. If using rocks, it's very important to choose rocks large enough that the water won't wash them away during storm events (there are ways to calculate the size of the rock needed).

Flowing water can cut deep gullies if its energy is not dissipated. Here, water from an inside ditch is eroding the road edge.

Here, water from a rolling dip was eroding the road edge. Rocks and concrete bags were carefully placed to stop the erosion.

Fish-Friendly Stream Crossings

We have all heard a lot about the need to save the fish, particularly salmon and steelhead. Roads, and particularly where roads cross watercourses, have long been and continued to be a focus of attention for reducing excessive sediment delivery into watercourses. (It's a little-known fact that fish need some sediment in the water to replenish the gravels that move downstream over time. So some sediment is a good thing, though we know that much of a good thing is detrimental.) So what can you do to make your roads more fish-friendly?

First, remember that culverts are dams, and they all fail eventually. So when you put a culvert in, figure out where the water will go when it *does* fail. You might do a little extra roadwork to ensure when the failure occurs that the water will cut a channel right over the top of the culvert, rather than running down and cutting a new channel in it and moving massive amounts of dirt into the stream.

Second, if there are fish in your creek, ensure they can get past your culvert. You might make sure there is a resting pool on the downhill side so the fish can rest before swimming up the culvert. Make the gradient gentle, so the water is moving slowly enough to enable the fish to swim against the current inside the pipe. And place the culvert low enough so that the water inside the pipe will be deep enough for the fish to swim through. Finally, if your culvert is a long one, check out culverts that have baffles inside. These baffles give the fish a chance to rest inside the pipe without being carried out by the current.

Third, for crossings of watercourses that don't have fish, install rolling dips instead of culverts where possible. Wherever you can substitute a rolling dip for a culvert, you are avoiding future problems by not putting in one of those "dams" that will eventually fail and deliver sediment to downstream watercourses.

Bear in mind that sediment can come as easily from the road to a private residence, a vineyard, a county road or a state highway as easily as it can come from a logging road. And remember that fish have a lot of challenges besides sediment they are facing, such as reduced summer flows from diversion for human uses and predation by marine mammals.

Financial assistance for roadwork may be available through the CFIP program. Also, a guide entitled *A Landowner's Guide to Building Forest Access Roads* is available to landowners. Call the Helpline, 800-738-8733 for more information on either of these resources.

Road Surface Drainage

When you are constructing or maintaining a road, an important decision is whether to outslope or inslope. An outsloped road drops very gently from the inside to the outside so that water from the road surface flows off the road edge instead of running down the road. An insloped road drops gently to the inside, so that water from the road surface flows to an inside ditch. The water then flows in the ditch alongside the road to a point where it is piped across the road through a culvert.

Outsloping roads, which used to be done rarely, is now generally preferred to insloping. First, with no culverts or ditches to clean out, outsloped road are very low maintenance. Second, they get water off the road surface quickly, so the water doesn't have a chance to accumulate. This means that its potential to erode is low relative to channeling the water into a ditch where it can build up speed and volume…and therefore erosive potential. By not creating this source of fast-moving water, landowners can prevent potentially serious erosion problems.

Still, there are definitely situations in which insloping is preferred. If the road is cut through a wet area, for example, it can make sense to concentrate the water in an inside ditch. Another example is if soils are extremely erosive and outsloping would cause the water running across the road to cause excessive erosion along the road's edge. Also, outsloping can create unsafe driving conditions if people need to drive on the roads when they are icy and slippery.

If you do have an insloped road installed, be sure to regularly inspect both the ditches and the culverts. Clean them out at least once a year, and, if you can, go out again during storm periods. Also, be sure that the culverts are large enough. A 12"-diameter pipe should be considered as a minimum. To avoid creating gullies at the outlet of the culvert, choose the outflow location carefully. It should be in an area that can effectively dissipate the energy of the water flowing out of the pipe's outlet.

Ensuring proper road surface drainage is part of good forest stewardship. It means fewer expenses for the landowner by reducing erosion problems. It also helps keep creeks running clear by reducing the amount of sediment transported into them from the roads.

Avoid Inside Ditches

One day I was out with a landowner who lives in a forest subdivision. As we drove up the road to her 40 acres, my eye kept going back to the inside ditches along her main access road. The road was designed so that water would run into the ditch, down the hill, and flow through ditch-relief culverts.

Once a popular way of building roads, what we've found out is that inside ditches tend to be very high-maintenance. First, they need to be cleaned out periodically. This is because they have a tendency to fill up with sediment, both from sediment settling out of the water flowing through the ditch and also from dirt sloughing off of the road cutbank.

Second, inside ditches have a tendency to "downcut." The longer the "run" before the ditch is relieved, the faster the water flows. And the faster the water flows, the more it can cut down into the ditch itself, carrying the sediment it has just eroded.

Third, ditch-relief culverts require maintenance. The inlets need to be cleaned regularly so water can flow through freely. And culverts need to be checked to make sure that water is flowing into the inlet, not eroding road fill around the culvert inlet. When landowners can't or simply don't do this maintenance, the result can be a failed culvert that dumps large amounts of sediment directly into watercourses.

There are certainly places when inside ditches are still

preferred, but in general, conventional road-building wisdom is now to use alternatives like rolling dips whenever possible. This creates a road that is a little slower to drive but is very stable as well as easy and inexpensive to maintain.

Inside ditches have a tendency to "downcut," as seen here.

The landowner whose property I visited saw for herself how the inside ditches were downcutting and transporting sediment. Fortunately, when she has her own roads put in, she can have it done in a way that will give her a road system that will have few worries or expenses.

69

Winter Use of Roads

All roads are not the same. This is especially important to remember when you are considering using a road in the wintertime, because not all roads are meant to be used year-round. To ensure that sediment is not transported from the road into creeks, road surfaces and watercourse crossings must be designed properly.

Three main types of roads are permanent, seasonal and temporary. A permanent road is designed for year-road use. It has special road surfacing material where needed, such as rock or lignin. Equally if not more important, a permanent road has watercourse crossings (such as rolling dips, culverts, or bridges) designed that will accommodate floods that occur once every 50 or 100 years.

A seasonal road is designed for use during part of the year. Specifically, it is meant for travel in the non-winter and perhaps, in areas with hard freezes, when the road surface is frozen. Typically there is no special road surfacing. Seasonal roads, like permanent roads, have crossings designed to handle 50 or 100-year storm events. Often landowners or land managers can use ATVs, but not trucks or cars, on seasonal roads during the winter.

Finally, there are temporary roads. If these have culverts at all, they are only large enough to handle the amount of water expected during the period of use, which is only a few months. And culverts are pulled out before the beginning of winter. Like seasonal roads, they have no special road surfacing.

It's important to understand what kind of road you have and if it is OK to use it for access in the winter when things are wet. If a road wasn't designed at a high enough standard to handle traffic and keep sediment out of watercourses in the winter, then

Use of this road in the winter created deep ruts in the road surface. Winter use of roads not designed for year-round use can result in damage to the road and delivery of sediment to watercourses.

driving on it when it is wet can cause serious rilling, gullying, and other erosion problems that can muddy your waters and erode the road itself.

If you have a temporary or seasonal road that you want or need to use as a permanent road, consider spending some dollars to upgrade it.

Part IV -- Forests, You, Me and Them – We *are* Interconnected

Forestry, Forest Conversion, & Conservation

Endangered Species and California's Wood Imports

"I heard something worse that I had dreamed. I knew California was a substantial net importer of wood, but last night I heard we are an 80% net importer of wood. Now what's the ethics of that?" This was the comment of University of California Berkeley professor Bill Libby, addressing participants of a forestry conference in Sacramento in 2001.

The figures I have heard over the past few years range from 66-80%, but the fact is that here in California we *do* import the vast majority of the wood that we consume. Having recently traveled across eastern and central Canada and through much of the US, let me offer my opinion that here in California we have some of the most productive, most beautiful, and most resilient forestland that there is. The thought that we import wood, for example, from Canadian forests that experience very harsh winters and have much slower growth rates than our woods on the coast, is a very unsettling one.

That thought became even more unsettling after hearing Professor Libby's talk. He has done research to quantify what the impact is of this export of our demand for wood. His research shows that for every 100 acres of forestland we set aside in California and take out of timber production, we cause the extinction of one species somewhere else in the world, or at the very least, the timetable for extinction for that species is moved significantly forward.

The situation is different in coastal redwood forests, with their mild weather, plentiful rainfall, and the redwood's ability to stump-sprout. In these exceptionally productive forests, Libby's research shows that it takes the removal of only 33-50 acres from timber production to cause or significantly hasten the extinction of a species elsewhere. He did note that by changing the parameters of the model, the number of acres changes. But the basic premise is solid – our wood imports impact forests elsewhere.

This raises a critical question – When we make decisions about how our forests will be managed, do we choose to consider only the forests in our own backyard, or do we include in our vision the forests of our global community?

A bird's-eye view of the Klamath National Forest.

The Three Legs of Sustainability – Ecological, Social, and Economic

The word "sustainability" means different things to different people. My own ideas of sustainability in terms of forest management have been influenced from work on Forest Stewardship Council certifications, where the three legs of sustainability are emphasized: ecological, social, and economic.

The basic idea is that in order to be truly sustainable, a forest management system must be sustainable over the long term in all three of these areas. Just as a three-legged stool needs legs of equal strength to function properly, so does forest management. For example, if management provides well for ecological sustainability but doesn't provide sufficient economic incentive, the land use will change, perhaps being converted to non-forest uses. Or, if workers and the local community receive strong economic benefits by engaging in management so intensive that it's not ecologically sustainable, the system won't survive over the long term.

Ecological sustainability looks at natural systems and how our actions affect them. This includes obvious issues like rotation age and wildlife habitat, as well as less obvious issues like proper maintenance of roads, ensuring genetic diversity, and monitoring and assessment.

Social issues cover a broad range of topics. On the level of individuals, it can mean taking measures that treat workers and community members fairly, or having effective conflict resolution measures in place. On a broader level, it includes things like payment of taxes and compliance with local, regional, national and even international laws and treaties.

Economic sustainability is largely about seeing that the dollars add up. There must be sufficient revenue for an operation to remain financially viable and have enough for reinvestment. Doing so allows the operation to pay for measures needed to ensure ecological and social sustainability.

The ways to create sustainable systems are as varied as forest ecosystems themselves. But although they vary, there is a compelling argument to be made that systems that are sustainable in the long term have one thing in common – a strong foundation in the three legs of sustainability.

NIMBY Forests and Forestry

One day a high-school student named Carla was doing research for a school project and called my office with a very simple question. "Do we grow more wood than we cut in California?" The answer is of course "yes," but I wanted some firm numbers to back up that assertion.

A few phone calls confirmed that yes, indeed, we grow about twice the volume of wood that we harvest in the state. But what was startling was how far out of balance our level of consumption is with either what we grow or what we harvest.

We Californians consume four times what we harvest in the state. And we consume twice what we grow. Even if we cut all of our annual growth, we would only have met half of our demand.

Only 25% of the wood we consume comes from our "backyard" forests—those in the state of California. What do we know about forests and forestry in California? We know we have the strictest forest practice regulations in the country, and arguably in the world. We also know that we have in the coastal redwood zone some of the most productive and resilient forests in the world.

And what do we know about the vast quantities of wood we import? It comes from outside the state, sometimes from outside the country, from "Not-In-My-Back-Yard" Forests. What we consumers know about those forests and, more importantly, how they are managed is very little, if anything at all.

The fact is those forests are almost certainly not as carefully managed as forests here in California. There will always be exceptions, and there is, for example, excellent forestry practiced all over the world by landowners and land managers under independent third-party certification. But California sets a much higher bar for forestry practices than other states and other countries.

It's time we examine the ethics of importing 75% of the wood we consume.

The Threat of Forestland Conversion

A workshop of forestry and land conservation professionals in Santa Rosa June of 2003 focused on how to keep our state's forests intact and productive in the face of pressures to convert forestland to non-forest uses. The two primary threats that discussed were vineyard conversion and, equally if not more important, population pressure.

California's population of some 34 million is growing quickly. It's expected to grow by about a third in the next twenty years and nearly double by 2040.

What does this mean for our forests? It's very likely that many people will be seeking small and large parcels of forestland for private residences and retreats. This will do two things as more and more people buy a limited amount of land.

First, it will decrease the size of existing forest holdings and increase many different kinds of impacts on the land. When one family owns and lives on 5,000 acres, there is relatively little human impact. But if the area is split into 50 parcels of 100 acres each, local wildlife, watercourses, etc. will bear the effects of 50 families. A few examples of impacts include erosion resulting from more roads, fragmentation of habitat caused by openings for homes and other structures, and degradation of high-quality habitat by the activity and noise that are part of the daily life of humans and our domestic animals.

The second potential impact will be pressure to convert productive forest to unmanaged land. The likely results of such a conversion are several, but two stand out as especially important. When forests go completely unmanaged, fuels build up and increase the risk of catastrophic fire. Second, when productive forests lay idle, our demand for wood products is met from other states and countries that likely have less strict environmental protections than we have in California.

Getting the Incentives Right

A friend of mine often comments, "It's all about getting the incentives right." What he means is that it's more likely someone will do some particular thing if they have a positive incentive to do so. Looking at it another way, if people have a disincentive to do something good, it becomes less likely they will. My friend applies this idea to everything from childrearing to explaining the success or failure of government subsidies.

We can see this dynamic at work in the management of forests in California. Before the 1970s, California had an "ad valorem" tax on timber. That meant landowners had to pay taxes each year on trees they *didn't* cut. And if they cut a certain percentage of the volume of timber they had, they received a tax break for some years into the future. Landowners therefore had two very strong incentives to cut a lot of trees.

Predictably, lands were harvested very heavily, and one can argue very persuasively that it was in large part due to the taxation system. One elderly landowner tells the story of her family getting together and making the financially very difficult decision to not cut a prized grove of old-growth redwood. The grove stands today, but its survival came at a high financial cost to the family.

Fortunately, the taxation system was changed in the 1970s, and now landowners are taxed on the timber harvested. But today's forest landowners today are seeing a different kind of set of incentives and disincentives.

The disincentive today is against doing any kind of active land management. With plan costs typically in the tens of thousands of dollars, increasing risks of lawsuits from members of the public who may or may not understand and/or agree with the management objectives, and a virtual stranglehold of state and federal regulation, many landowners are choosing not to manage their property, even for fire risk reduction.

At the same time, there is a strong economic incentive to subdivide forest lands for residential parcels. The smaller the parcel, the more traveled roads, wildlife habitat fragmentation, and habitat degradation there will be.

If we are to maintain healthy forests and wildlife populations, we need to work harder to get the incentives right. We need to recognize and reward landowners who are good stewards of their property. We need to provide the incentives to encourage landowners to be good stewards. We need a little more honey and a lot less vinegar.

Private Property and Public Trust Values

At a training session on marbled murrelets put on by the US Fish and Wildlife Service and the California Department of Fish and Game, three wildlife biologists spoke about what is known and what isn't known about these birds and their habitat.

The nesting habitat of the birds was discussed, of which one key element is large limbs in conifers, including Douglas-fir, redwood, and western hemlock. The birds use as nests large limbs, an average of 13 inches in diameter at the bole of the tree, in the upper 60% of the tree. Also discussed was what little is known about the life history of the bird as well as the survey protocol and protection measures.

After the biologists had given their presentations, foresters began asking questions and expressing concerns. A primary concern that surfaced is the recurring question of the rights of people to utilize their lands as they see fit versus the power of the government to restrict those activities in the pursuit of protecting public trust values.

Let's look at an example of the interaction of the murrelet and a forest landowner. This not-so-hypothetical landowner has on his 40-acre property a sustained yield plan (NTMP) for which he paid about $10,000. He is a resident landowner who wants to grow big trees, keep the residual older trees (they are, after all, "cool"), maintain good aesthetics, while making enough to pay the cost of his management plan, the property taxes, to keep his roads in good shape, and to have a little profit besides. The plan is certified by an independent third party as being ecologically well managed. One could hardly ask for a better steward of the land.

Yet if a murrelet were to decide to take up residence on his property, the landowner's ability to actively manage the land would be severely curtailed. Immediately a no-cut zone would be established that would cover 6.5 acres, preventing any harvesting at all. Additionally, seasonal restrictions would kick in that would cover an additional 183 acres, encompassing his entire parcel.

There is, therefore, a strong disincentive for this landowner to grow the big, old trees he would really like to have. The incentive is to harvest more heavily than he really wants to in order to ensure that murrelets don't move in. This particular landowner continues to grow the big trees, and by doing so he risks his ability to continue active management in the future.

We all want the biological diversity, clean water, and other functions of a healthy forest from which we as a society benefit. At the same time, small forest landowners have made significant financial investments in their property (tens to hundreds of thousands of dollars), and many have made significant further investments by paying $10,000-$50,000 to put a management plan on that property. Simply taking away their private property rights and their ability to recoup costs and make a modest profit will result in the subdivision and conversion of forest land. We already see this happening, and we need to find a better way.

Rights and Responsibilities

We all know that with rights come responsibilities. This also holds true when we talk about forest land, public trust values, private landowners, and the public.

A forest is a precious resource that provides many benefits to the public, some of which include: clean water, production of oxygen, wildlife habitat, nutrient cycling, as well as aesthetic and even spiritual values. From a forest in timber production, we add to the list wood and wood products.

Members of the public assert they have a right to these benefits derived from private forests. While the vast majority of the public does not own forest land, they recognize that the forest has public trust values which need to be protected for the greater good. Various arms of government are charged with protecting these rights through environmental legislation.

Forest landowners assert they have a right to manage their lands. They have made significant investment in the purchase of their holdings. They have annual maintenance costs, and often landowners spend a lot of time and money improving their property. Many view their holdings as an investment and claim their right to work for a return on that investment.

So what are the corresponding responsibilities?

Private forest landowners have a responsibility to take reasonable steps to ensure that the public trust values are protected. To this end, they comply with environmental legislation such as the Forest Practice Rules, CEQA, CESA and ESA. In so doing, forest landowners bear significant costs for regenerating the forest, surveying for and protecting wildlife habitat and archaeological resources, as well as fixing and upgrading old roads.

The public and the government that represents the public have the responsibility to take reasonable steps to ensure that private forest landowners with productive holdings can actively manage that property in the black. Requirements and regulations should not be so expensive and burdensome that landowners cannot financially afford to comply. Watershed assessment, the long-term collection and dissemination of data on a watershed scale, as well as monitoring, are beyond the financial resources of typical forest landowners and should be paid for with public dollars.

The public also has the responsibility to balance its consumption of wood products with the level of harvest it finds acceptable.

Finally, if protecting the public trust values means the landowner's ability to manage his or her property is significantly reduced, then should the public not be responsible for compensating the landowner for that loss?

Forest Conversion and Edge Effects

On a trip to the United Kingdom in January, I spoke with several people about the issue of conversion of forestland to other uses. Some said that in the UK there is more conversion of farmland to forest than of forest to other uses. But others maintained that, at least in certain areas, the loss of forestland was a serious issue, citing anecdotal accounts of decreases in certain bird populations. Whatever the case over there, in California there can be little doubt that conversion of forestland to uses such as vineyards and residential subdivisions is a serious issue.

The most obvious impacts are the loss of forested acres and the fragmentation of remaining habitat. These impacts are relatively intuitive. From the perspective of wildlife, fewer acres of course mean less habitat. And in areas where remaining habitat is fragmented, how those fragments are or aren't connected influences how effectively different species are able to use the remaining forest.

But other important impacts can arise from the creation of more forest edges, or places where the forest ends. Such places might include a natural meadow, a road, or an area cleared for a homesite or a vineyard.

Researchers have studied the "edge effect" and found that in the adjacent forest there are changes in available sunlight, temperature, and windspeed. Apart from these impacts, it is certain that there are also changes in the level of noise and general activity that occur when people and their household animals move into or next to a forest.

While some of these changes might seem slight to us, they may be significant for wildlife or botanical species. Different species have different tolerances for changes of various kinds to their habitat, changes that can come from either the loss of forestland or the creation of relatively more forest edges.

Deer in a meadow at dusk near Rockpile Road in Sonoma County. Sizes of forest holdings in this area now range from about 160 acres to over 5,000 acres.

Forestry and Conservation

Do forestry and conservation go hand in hand? To my forester friends, the answer is "Well of course!" To many others, however, the answer seems less obvious.

In answering this question, it's important to distinguish between "conservation" and "preservation." They are not at all the same thing. Conservation is the wise use of resources. The objective is long-term sustained use of resources, making sure they maintain their productivity in the long term, while also providing for compatible human uses and benefit. Preservation, by contrast, excludes human intervention and management.

So if conservation – wise use of our resources – is the goal, how do we get there? Forests are dynamic systems, always growing and changing. It is reasonable to assume that the people who are best able to help us define workable conservation strategies and achieve conservation goals will understand the dynamics of the forest, and also that they will have experience and education in land management, silviculture, forest ecosystems, wildlife, ecology, soils, etc. In short, we need people with the kind of education, experience, and perspective that a forester has.

We also need landowners who know what they want to achieve and are willing to make the economic or other contributions needed to realize their goals. Whether public or private, it is important for landowners to determine what their goals are for a property, make sure the goals are realistic in terms of social, ecological, and economic realities, and then find a forester who understands, respects, and will work toward those goals.

One final thought – there is no free lunch here. Good management of a forest, whether or not it is managed for commercial forestry, isn't free. There are recurring costs for taxes and road upkeep, in addition to paying the forester or other land manager. Good forestry can provide some or all of the income needed for good conservation. If that income doesn't come from forestry, it will have to come from somewhere else.

Lake Arrowhead's State of Emergency

What happens when a severely overcrowded forest faces several years of drought? The unfortunate answer is being played out in Lake Arrowhead, about 100 miles from Los Angeles, where Governor Davis declared a state of emergency in 2003.

The problem? Bark beetles. Lots and lots of them. Normally, a healthy tree can ward off bark beetles. It does this by producing sap, which pitches the beetles out or simply drowns them. But many of the trees in Lake Arrowhead have been unable to do this for two reasons.

First, the trees are tremendously overcrowded. In the absence of natural wildfires or mechanical thinnings, for years the densely crowded trees have been competing with each other for sunlight, water, and nutrients. Just as your overall health would decline if you had to split every meal with another person or two, so does a tree's health decline when crowded in with too many other trees. The end result is that it has less energy to produce the sap it depends on to fight off beetles.

Second, the area has experienced five years of drought. This has been a significant additional stress on the overcrowded trees, making it more difficult for them to produce quantities of sap adequate to fight off the bark beetles. The result is that tremendous numbers of trees, including healthy ones, are succumbing to the beetles.

Reports peg the number of dead trees in excess of one million, and the problem is far from solved. Homeowners are spending tens of thousands of dollars, in some cases taking out loans, to pay for the removal of dead trees that would threaten their homes if a wildfire were to occur.

What is happening now is Lake Arrowhead is a wake-up call to us all that a "no-management" approach to tending our forests can have very costly consequences, both for the forest and for us.

Wildfire Protection and the Interface Zone

At a forestry conference in 2002, the California Department of Forestry's Director Andrea Tuttle addressed the fact that as people move into urban-rural "Interface Zones" and build homes, fire protection becomes more difficult and more expensive. She estimated that some $20 million is needed statewide to provide adequate fire protection in the areas the state is responsible for (not including federal lands). The burning question is, who will pay for those services?

The Interface Zone, or I-Zone, refers to where urban and rural areas meet and interface. This can take many forms. It includes, for example, the area of the Oakland hills fire in the 90s. It also includes areas where large ranches have been split up into small parcels and homes built on those parcels.

Homeowners are building in the Interface Zone of the forested hills above Mendocino County's Ukiah valley.

Firefighting needs and strategies change once an area becomes populated. For example, in a wildland area, the best strategy might be to contain a fire at a ridgetop, letting the mountainside burn all the way up to that ridge and stopping the fire there. But add homes and people to that same mountainside, and the highest priorities become saving human life and minimizing damage to structures.

Fire-fighting agencies have limited personnel and equipment and can be faced with tough decisions about where to put their resources. CDF has many agreements with local districts and agencies to provide fire-fighting services and facilitate quickly moving people and equipment to where they are needed. But with so many people in I-Zone areas requiring fire protection and with our high fuel loading, the existing system is strained.

An important question raised by CDF Director Tuttle is whether or not landowners are paying their own way when it comes to the fire protection services they rely on. And if not, who should pay—the landowners, the local community, the county, or the state? What we know with certainly is that more dollars are needed to provide fire protection and fire-fighting services. Where those dollars should come from will likely be a hotly debated issue.

We Affect the Forest

Keeping the Forest a Forest

When you think about what a forest wants and needs, what comes to mind?

Some of the most important inputs for the forest we don't have much control over. Water, for example, is probably the first thing that comes to mind. Or perhaps you think of sunlight or nutrients in the soil.

Apart from sometimes fertilizing trees, there's little we can do about providing any of those inputs. But there are two important things that we can do to help the forest.

The first is to practice good management. Now I know that people can argue for hours over whether or not a particular project is "good" management or not. Suffice it to say that management can take many forms – thinning, pruning, fuels reduction, planting, stream bank stabilization, or other restoration work. What is good for you and your property will be determined by your personal goals for the land, your land ethic, and the condition that the forest is in now. The important thing to remember is that doing nothing is generally not good management. Forests are dynamic systems, and good stewardship means active involvement.

Second, perhaps the most important action you can take is to resolve that your forest will remain as a forest. With management costs increasing, the prices of timber decreasing, and California's population rising, there are tremendous pressures to sell forest land for development into residential subdivision, vineyards, or other uses. The decision to keep a forest as a forest despite these pressures is in many cases becoming as difficult as it is important.

This meadow is located just off a main access road not far from a major highway. With its easy access and beautiful view, it is a prime example of an area at risk of being converted to a private residence. If that happens, people may bring pets, a septic system, and perhaps even a small vineyard to this meadow.

Our Ecological Footprint

"Ecological footprint," "life-cycle assessment," "environmental footprint" -- these are terms used to describe the impact of our consumption of material goods on the environment. We all use resources, though usually our awareness of them begins when we break out the checkbook and ends with the trip to the dump, or when the check is cashed. In other words, we usually think more in terms of a financial footprint than an ecological footprint.

To evaluate an ecological footprint, a lot of "Before" and "After" questions need to be considered. "Before" questions focus on the making and marketing of a product. What resources were used to create the product? Where was it produced? How much energy was used in transporting it to the store shelf? What laws to protect workers the environment did or did not have to followed? "After" questions focus on use and disposal. For example, is the product recyclable? How much energy does it take to recycle it? How many years will the gases or chemicals used to make the product persist in the environment, and with what effects?

When looking at forest products and their substitutes, it's important to ask these questions. If we buy imported from Canada, for example, that creates a much bigger ecological footprint than if we buy wood produced here in California. One obvious reason is the cost of transporting the product. A less intuitive reason is that environmental laws are much stricter here in California. If we buy products made at lower cost because environmental standards are lower, we end up in effect exporting bad forestry practices. And if we choose to buy products that substitute for wood, we need to consider as part of the ecological footprint the energy, water, fuel, chemicals, etc. that go into producing and transporting that material, as well as the life expectancy and recyclability of the resource.

These are questions we need to think about even when our pocketbook does not force us to. Sound like a brain-bender? It can be. But the more honestly we can face the true ecological footprint of our individual choices, the more we empower ourselves to make decisions that are truly consistent with our beliefs.

Inactive Forest Management

All of our forestland in California is managed. This includes several kinds of active management that readily come to mind, such as planting, harvesting, fighting fires (remember that even the decision whether or not to fight a fire is a management decision), erosion control, and restoration work. But it also includes "inactive management."

Inactive management has a profound effect on the forest. It is a conscious decision that nothing will be done in order to "let nature take its course." The belief is that the forest will revert to a functional, sustainable, ecologically well-balanced ecosystem. The factor that is overlooked is fire. The results are overgrown forests and forests that shift from a mixture of species that love light and those that love shade to forests heavily skewed to those species that can survive in and reproduce in shaded conditions.

Our forests evolved with and depended on fire to keep them healthy and diverse. Fires thinned out stands of trees, providing sunlight for sun-loving species and leaving more resources for trees that remained, in effect giving the survivors more food on their dinner plates. When fire is excluded, as it has been for decades by those brave men and women we rely on to protect our homes and property, forests become overcrowded. They become stressed, more vulnerable to insect and disease attacks. So long as we suppress fires, and there is no doubt that we will continue to do so, we must understand that we cannot by doing nothing successfully return forests to the ecological balance of the times before humans began manipulating them.

As an interesting note, I visited two properties along the central coast in areas hit hard by the Sudden Oak Death syndrome. These were properties that had been actively managed, one for over 30 years, under selection silviculture (harvesting of individual trees and small groups of trees). What I noticed was that in surrounding areas, there were a lot of dead tanoaks. On the properties I visited, there were very few dead tanoaks.

Now it may just be coincidence that the stands with fewer trees had less evidence of this disease, and it is possible that the disease will eventually hit those stands as hard as it has hit surrounding stands. But it just may be that the trees that have more sunlight, water and nutrients available are better able to fight off the disease. We know so little about the disease, it is hard to say. What we do know is that crowded trees are more stressed than thinned-out trees.

The point is that it is important to understand that inactive management is a form of management. Whether under active or inactive management, all forestland in California is managed.

Practicing For-Profit Forestry the Sustainable Way

During a break at a workshop, a fellow participant approached me and asked why foresters have to work for companies that are for-profit. Why, he asked, can't they just manage forests non-commercially, like parks? My short answer was that foresters want to make a living practicing forestry, and there's not enough money to put all our forests into parks and pay for their management even if we wanted to.

But the longer answer is that it is certainly possible for a company to manage a forest very well while making a profit. In fact, making a profit may help ensure that a forest will be managed well, as opposed to being divided up into small parcels whose the owners largely neglect dealing with everyday issues such as roads and fuel loading.

One of my favorite examples of a for-profit company that manages its lands well is Redtree Properties in Santa Cruz. Certified by SmartWood as having ecologically, socially, and economically sustainable management, they've focused for decades on producing high-quality trees and habitat by doing single-tree selection harvests.

Their head forester, Jim Greig, comments, "The owners are managing for the long term, not short-term exploitation. We've been working for 30 years to improve the quality and quantity of the forest, and I think its current condition shows that we've been successful. "

I've seen their property and have to agree. So does the manager of the county park adjacent to Redtree. The park acquired its land from the Redtree owners 30 years ago, and since then they've let nature take its course. The park manager comments that Redtree's management provides an excellent example for other landowners, and that in his opinion, the Redtree property looks better than the park land.

The owners of Redtree do love their forest, but at the same time they are also very savvy. If the company doesn't make money, they know that their thousands of acres of beautiful redwood land only a few miles from Silicon Valley is worth an absolute fortune.

So why do the Redtree foresters work for a for-profit company? Because they are able to keep a large tract of forestland intact, prevent it from being subdivided, maintain contiguous wildlife habitat, provide local residents recreational and educational opportunities, and provide high-quality lumber. In short, because they enjoy being an integral part of a terrific model for sustainable forestry.

Shaded Fuelbreak at RVOEP

The Redwood Valley Outdoor Education Project (RVOEP) is sporting a new demonstration of a shaded fuelbreak. If you've ever wondered what a shaded fuelbreak is or what it looks like, visit the RVOEP site, just north of Ukiah in Mendocino County, and take a look.

What you'll see on one side of the road going into the site is the unmanaged stand. The result of many years of inactive management, it is thick with live trees with many low-hanging limbs, dead trees and brush, and a lot of live brush. If you imagine a fire in this forest, it's easy to see how it would climb up into the tree canopy. You can also easily imagine how difficult it would be to fight a fire in such dense vegetation.

On the other side of the road you'll see the shaded fuel break. The first thing you'll notice is that you can see through the forest. The brush has been cleared, and dead trees and shrubs were removed. Live trees were thinned out, and those that remain were limbed as high up as the crew could reach with pole saws.

The project site before the fuelbreak was put in shows dense vegetation with many low-hanging limbs and dead material.

The same view after fuels reduction. Not the removal of tree limbs and ground fuels. The pile of branches on the left was later removed. The background shows an area not thinned.

The idea behind a shaded fuel break is that many of the ground, ladder, and crown fuels are removed while leaving well-spaced live trees that shade the area. Besides reducing the amount of material that burns, shaded fuelbreaks eliminate "ladder" fuels that give fire an easy way to climb from the ground into the tree canopy. They also open up spaces in the canopy so that the heat from a fire can escape, rather than being trapped by dense layers of limbs.

The RVOEP site is open to the public. The best times to visit are Saturday through Monday, weekdays after 2 pm, or anytime after school is out for the summer. Park outside of the gate and walk in. The site is located at 8301 Pinecrest Drive. Take Pinecrest Drive, opposite from the Redwood Valley elementary school, about 1/2 mile to the RVOEP gate.

Exporting Demand

While working on a forestry job in China in 2002, I had some interesting conversations with Chinese foresters. It seems that forestry in California and China have at least two important issues in common – the exporting of demand for wood and the consequent export of poor forestry practices.

In China, only about half of the nation's demand for wood is met domestically. The other half comes from many countries, but the primary source is Siberia. Because so much of the logging and transport is done illegally, there are no reliable figures on how much is imported, but it is widely recognized to be a very significant amount.

Several years ago, after severe floods on the Yangtze River, the Chinese government dramatically cut back the level of permitted harvests. Some harvests are still allowed, but the country's demand for wood is high, and so vast quantities are imported. This has accelerated over-harvesting using poor forestry practices in Siberia, which has become an increasing concern for international conservation organizations. There is no clear solution for either decreasing China's demand for imports or for improving forestry practices in Siberia.

There are two similarities between the situation in California and that in China. First, we also import significant amounts of wood to meet our demand. We import relatively more than China, however, meeting an estimated 70% of our needs through imports. Second, we are none too selective about where the wood we use comes from. Price is the overriding factor, and little consideration is given to the forest management of the areas in which the wood is grown. We now bring in wood from Washington and Oregon, Canada, as well as plantations as far away as Chile or New Zealand. Most of us know little to nothing about how forests are managed in those areas.

Having seen plantation management in both the southeast of the United States and in China, my own opinion is that what foresters in California do to manage forests on a sustainable basis and to protect non-timber resources such as water quality and wildlife habitat far exceeds what foresters elsewhere do. No system is perfect, but ours works better to protect the environment than what I've seen in other states and countries. Our system, I would argue, works better than those used in places from which we import wood.

Declining Harvests – The Right Road?

"You know what's been happening with the small landowner? We're losing them." That was the remark of a forester who has worked for a small family mill for many years, commenting on changes in forest management in Mendocino County.

The numbers bear out his observation. In 2002, harvests from Mendocino County once again declined, down nearly 20% from 2001 levels. Those numbers have been falling sharply since 1996, when harvests in our county were nearly three times what they were in 2002.

Part of the decline is due to that fact that small landowners can't afford to have harvest plans written. It's not uncommon to hear stories of small landowners spending $30,000 on a harvest plan, sometimes without ending up with an approved plan. And even with an approved plan, many landowners would have to harvest so heavily just to recover plan costs that they figure it's not worth their while to do so.

Another reason for low harvest levels is that the price of logs is very low. The average price statewide, reported by the state Board of Equalization, dropped significantly between 2000 and 2002. We now import the vast majority of the wood we use in California from other states and countries, and cheap production elsewhere is driving log prices down.

A third factor is that many new landowners aren't interested in harvesting. Many have bought small acreages (often that have already been heavily logged) as private retreats. A few do limited management like fuels reduction around homesites or emergency repairs on roads. But for the most, the dynamic forests that make up these properties are left unmanaged.

As population increases, more people move into the woods, building new roads to access their property. Note that this photo shows two different roads accessing private homes.

The risk is, of course, twofold. For areas that remain in forest, the risk is that a no management approach will result in high fuel loading leading to catastrophic fire, as well as sediment delivery to watercourses from unmaintained roads. But in areas where population pressures are intensifying, the greater risk is that our forests will continue to be converted to non-forest uses as landowners find they can make handsome profits by selling off pieces of the family forest.

The question really is, what do we want our forests, as well as those not in our own backyard, to look like in two or three generations? And are we on the road to getting there?

Impacts of Non-Forestry Activities

Practicing foresters can tell you all about the requirements of the California's Forest Practice Rules when it comes to regenerating a stand after harvest. If there aren't enough trees left after harvest, landowners are required to plant and, if necessary, replant, until they have adequate regeneration of trees.

But other, non-forestry land-use activities not only allow for the clearing of forestland without replanting, but also permit the permanent conversion of the forest to other uses. These activities have little to no oversight or assessment of cumulative impacts. And these activities are being pursued at an increasing rate.

Two of the most common and significant activities are clearing for agricultural purposes and for developing homesites (as well as roads to those homesites). When on coniferous forestland, there is some level of oversight by the Department of Forestry. But on oak woodlands, it's a different story.

Greg Giusti of the University of California Cooperative Extension has put together a very interesting slide presentation pointing out these inconsistencies in environmental laws and policies when it comes to California's oak woodlands. One very powerful slide shows an oak woodland in the foreground, and in the background, just on the other side of a creek, is a conifer-dominated hillside. He notes that a landowner wishing to harvest trees from the conifer area would be subject to the high cost and strict environmental review of a Timber Harvest Plan. The same landowner wanting to cut the oak woodland and put in a homesite or a vineyard, for example, would have virtually no requirements on road building, stream protection, etc.

"There is a double standard," Giusti asserts. He began to look into this issue when local foresters expressed to him their frustration at seeing oak woodlands clearcut for vineyards.

Oak woodlands, like coniferous forests, provide important wildlife habitat and spawning grounds for anadromous fish. Both forestry and non-forestry activities need to address protecting habitat by, for example, maintaining riparian habitat and reducing sediment transport from roads. The solution is not to broaden the application of the Forest Practice Rules, which are widely recognized as being an extremely onerous and a broken system. But we do need to find creative, workable solutions to ensure that all segments of society share the responsibility for and the cost of the recovery of our natural resources.

Oak woodlands are found both above and below this vineyard in Mendocino County.

Forest Health

Too Many Trees for a Healthy Forest?

The fact that we have very low harvest levels in California means that we are growing far more than we are harvesting. This begs the question, are we growing healthy forests?

In too many cases, the answer is clearly no. Many of our forests are overcrowded and stressed, offering unbroken seas of fuel for wildfires. The reason is, of course, that when we suppress fires for our safety, we alter the natural fire cycles that our forests evolved with.

One summer I drove from Chicago back home to California. There were lots of hardwoods to see in Nebraska, a state that proudly proclaims itself Home of Arbor Day. In Wyoming there were more conifers, but they were much smaller and slow-growing than what I am accustomed to seeing. In the high deserts there were patches of juniper that towered a full fifteen or twenty feet above the sagebrush. But it was not until I drove into the Sierras that I began to feel back at home, among the tall and majestic conifers.

The only trouble was, they didn't look good. Many of the trees had small diameters and were crowded together. Just as I was thinking, "This really needs to be thinned before a fire comes through," I rounded a corner to see an entire hillside that was brown. A hot fire had come through and killed everything from the ridge down as far as I could see, leaving nothing green that was visible from the road.

A few years ago when I was running the Forest Stewardship Helpline, a forester from Washington State called after having dropped his daughter off at college in California. "You people have a big problem down there," he said, clearly concerned. He proceeded to explain the mile after mile of overcrowded forest he had seen that was ripe for insect infestation, disease, and wildfire. I could only agree with him. He ended with, "Well, someone ought to do something about it."

He's right. Someone ought to do something about it. And it will take a lot of "someones" – a lot of us -- doing something to make a difference.

Sudden Oak Death

In April of 2002, top researchers put on a training session to help foresters and others identify and sample for *Phytophthora ramorum,* commonly known as Sudden Oak Death. The researchers stressed the importance of tracking this *Phytophthora* (which means "plant killer"), to help understand how it might be possible to slow its spread, adding that landowners and foresters need to keep an eye out for and report suspected occurrences.

As a first step, it's helpful to know where the disease has and hasn't been found. It hadn't, as of April 2002, been found in street trees or blue oaks. It has been found in forested communities and forest remnants, though it tends not to be in areas with very dense canopies. The disease is found in black oak, tanoak, coast live oak, bay laurel, bigleaf maple, buckeye, and Shreve's oak. It has also been found in manzanita, evergreen huckleberry, rhododendron, toyon, honeysuckle, Coffeeberry and arrowwood.

One of the challenges in identification is that the pathogen causes different symptoms in different hosts. In some species, like bay laurel or madrone, it attacks the foliage and/or twigs, creating discolored areas on the leaves. In these "foliar hosts," the host is not killed but plays a key role in spreading the disease. In other species, like live oak or black oak, it attacks the main stem of the tree, and you find cankers and often areas that are "bleeding" a thick, dark-red liquid. Trees whose stems are attacked usually are killed. In tanoak, which is one of the most susceptible species, the pathogen attacks the trees in both ways.

To complicate matters, there are other pathogens that can cause similar symptoms. So if you see cankers or spots on brush or trees, there's a good chance it's something other than Sudden Oak Death. There are telltale signs, however, such as the entire crown of an oak or tanoak suddenly dying. But even this is variable, and some oaks can take two or three years to die.

If you think you have infected trees, the only way to be sure it is Sudden Oak Death is to have someone come out to take a sample that will be tested in the lab. Spring is a good time to sample, as the dry conditions of summer and fall yield many false negative lab results.

Report suspected infections by contacting the County Agricultural Commissioner or the University of California Cooperative Extension. Ask about getting someone to come out and take a sample. For the latest information on this disease, visit www.suddenoakdeath.org.

Sudden Oak Death in Redwood and Doug-fir

The California Oak Mortality Task Force, which gives the official word on Sudden Oak Death Syndrome (SODS), announced in September of 2002 that the disease had been isolated on both redwood and Douglas-fir. The unanswered question, though, is exactly what that will mean for our forests.

Researchers found infected Doug-fir saplings in Sonoma County. They also found infected redwood saplings in Sonoma County's Jack London State Park and Henry Cowell State Park in Santa Cruz. There had not been, however, any confirmed instances of mature redwood or Doug-fir dying from SODS, and symptoms on redwoods were found only on leaves and small branches.

Researchers explain that some species tolerate the disease better than others. Some, like tanoak, are highly susceptible, while the symptoms for other species such as buckeye seem to be minor, limited to spots on leaves. The type and severity of symptoms can also vary with the age of a tree species. For example, drooping shoots are more common in young tanoak, while mature tanoak is more likely to show "bleeding" symptoms. What this means is that even though the disease was found on redwood and Doug-fir, we really don't know how severe the impact will be, or whether or not it will impact mature trees.

What can you do? Remember that this disease spreads by spores and cysts through the soil and the air. So avoid transporting soil from infected areas. If you walk or ride bikes on trails in areas that are infected, wash the dirt or mud off your shoes and vehicles. This is particularly important in wet weather when soil is muddy and more likely to stick to your shoes or tires. If you aren't sure if you are traveling to an infected area, take a minute to check the Oak Mortality Task Force's website, where you can view maps that show locations of the disease. It may take a little while to find what you need, but the information will be there, at www.suddenoakdeath.org.

Is It Sudden Oak Death? Think Horses, Not Zebras

They say that in medical school, students learn that they should first explore the most common possible cause of a particular ailment before assuming less common possible causes. For example, a doctor should look at the possibility that a person with a cough has a common cold before assuming the patient has tuberculosis. When you hear hooves, the students are told, think "horses" before you think "zebras."

That phrase came to mind when a landowner from northern Mendocino County brought in a dead sprig from a Douglas-fir tree and asked if it was killed by Sudden Oak Death. He had heard that researchers had found a Douglas-fir sapling in a park in Sonoma County that tested positive for Sudden Oak Death. And so he was thinking "zebras" (Sudden Oak Death) instead of "horses," (more common causes of tree mortality).

It's likely the mortality the landowner saw in his Douglas-fir was the result of insufficient water. We had had some dry years, and lack of water (water stress) can kill trees directly or indirectly by lowering its overall level of vigor and making it more susceptible to attacks by common insects and disease.

It's important to remember that just because you see the name of a tree or shrub on the list of species affected by Sudden Oak Death, that doesn't mean that your Douglas-fir or huckleberry is going to get infected and die. This is true for several reasons. First, the disease is limited geographically. Yes, the range is expanding, but there may well be areas that are simply unsuitable for the pathogen due to temperature or moisture conditions.

Second, the disease won't kill all the individuals of all species impacted by it. Many species, like the bay laurel, are foliar hosts that appear to be only carriers. They spread the disease but are rarely if ever killed by it. And for the species that can be killed by the disease, there appears to be some natural resistance. In Pine Pitch Canker, another tree disease in California, it's estimated that about 15% of the trees have good natural resistance.

It's too early to say how dramatically Sudden Oak Death will change our landscape, or what percentage of the effected oaks will have natural resistance. Certainly, many trees have died, and more will. But when you see a dead or dying tree in the range of Sudden Oak Death, think "horses" before you think "zebras."

About Your Home in the Woods

Defensible Space

If you live in the woods and aren't familiar with what "defensible space" is, it's likely you have some work to do around your house. "Defensible space" is the area in which you modify vegetation around your home or other structures. Reducing the amount and distribution of fuels makes it easier for firefighters to fight a wildfire.

How big should a defensible space be? In part it depends on the location of your structure. The easiest building to defend is one on flat ground. When a home is built on the edge of a hill so that a magnificent view can be enjoyed, the risk to the home from fire increases significantly. Fires move quickly uphill, preheating upslope fuels as they go. So if a home is on a hillside, the size of the defensible space zone will need to be relatively large.

The type and density of vegetation are also critical factors. The goal isn't to eliminate fuels (trees, brush, herbaceous vegetation and grasses) within the defensible space, but to break them into isolated islands. The point is to make it difficult for a fire to move from one island of fuel to another. It's also important to reduce fuel ladders, which are shrubs or low-hanging branches that would allow a fire burning on the ground to climb up into the crowns of trees.

In general, a defensible space should include areas within 100 feet or more from a structure, depending on the steepness of the slope. If you have a lot of trees within 150 feet of a legally permitted structure and need to thin them out, you can do so under a "fire exemption," filed with CDF. Also, remember to make your roads accessible to fire fighters by cutting back shrubs and low-hanging branches so that fire trucks can pass.

Material that you cut can be lopped and scattered, chipped, or piled and burned. If you burn piles, keep the piles small, and call Air Quality's burn information line before burning to make sure it's a permissive burn day.

An owner-builder in Mendocino County, this landowner has 40 acres of mixed conifer forest. Note that the house was strategically placed to take advantage of a large meadow down oo.slope from the structures.

Landscaping and Defensible Space

As you work on the landscaping around your house, keep in mind that landscaping is an important part of maintaining defensible space around your home and other buildings. Basically, you want to reduce fuels in three zones around your house or structure.

The innermost zone, within 30 feet of your house, should ideally be a greenbelt of low-growing, fire-resistant plants. If you do have trees, pruning dead branches to at least 10 or 15 feet. Irrigation and removal of accumulated leaf litter and other woody debris improve the effectiveness of this zone. Some examples of fire-resistant plants include western redbud, toyon, wild strawberry, oleander, and lilac. A more complete list, compiled by Bruce Hagan of CDF, is available from the Helpline.

The mid-zone, 30 to 70-150 feet from the house, should also contain mostly low-growing, fire-resistant plants. Some well-spaced, fire-resistant trees can be maintained. Plants in this zone should be drought tolerant, though periodic irrigation can reduce flammability.

More native vegetation can be maintained in the outermost zone, beyond 70-150 feet from the house. Dense brush as well as crowded trees should be thinned.

The U.C. Cooperative Extension has a nifty little publication called *A Property Owner's Guide to Reducing Wildfire Threat*. This excellent 6-page brochure provides lots of useful details about defensible space, including a short tree list classifying the trees as "Bark Sensitive to Fire" and "Bark Less Sensitive to Fire." The brochure is available through the Helpline at 800-738-8733.

Fuelbreaks and Lines of Defense

With the fires of summer just around the corner, it's a good time to start thinking about managing vegetation near your home. There's a lot of hard physical work involved in cutting, pruning, chipping or burning vegetation, so it really pays to look critically at where your efforts will be most effective and to concentrate your work there.

Think in terms of establishing "lines of defense." These will be areas that have little or no vegetation and that can be used to stop or significantly slow a spreading fire. Some examples of lines of defense you may already have include roads, lakes, ridges, or rocky outcrops. Note that the effectiveness of roads in stopping a fire is greatly increased when the fuels on either side of the road have been cut back or at least thinned out.

Under the Forest Practice Rules, there are two silvicultural prescriptions specifically designed to help you create these lines of defense. The first, which has been around for quite a few years, is the Fire Exemption. The exemption is available for cutting selected trees within 150 feet of a legally permitted structure. The stand left after harvest must not resemble a clearcut or a harvest in which seed or shelterwood trees (certain overstory trees) are removed. All slash from the harvesting must be treated within 45 days of the start of operations. Slash must be removed from within 100 feet of the structure, and slash between 100 and 150 feet from the structure must be removed, burned or chipped.

For projects that extend further from your home or other structure, you can commercially harvest your trees under a second, newer option, as a Fuelbreak/Defensible Space operation. The intent of this prescription is to allow landowners to create "shaded fuelbreaks" in which some trees and vegetation are removed while retaining significant stocking levels. The stand after harvest must meet stocking standards specified in the Forest Practice Rules.

Whether or not you are not planning to sell logs commercially, you can significantly reduce your risk of catastrophic fire by managing vegetation near your home to reduce fuels.

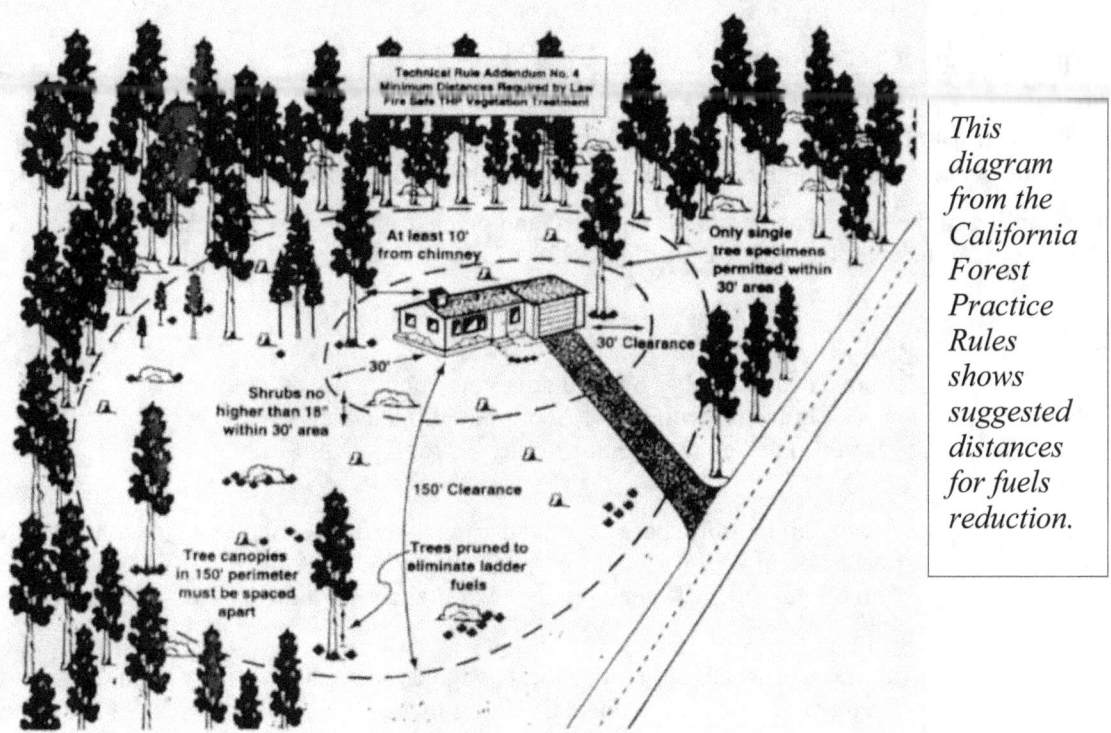

This diagram from the California Forest Practice Rules shows suggested distances for fuels reduction.

Fire, Your Home, and Baby Diapers?

What is the connection between fire, your home,2 and baby diapers? You read that right – baby diapers. The answer is that baby diapers have provided the inspiration for a new way to help protect your home from wildfire.

Back in the mid-1990s, an observant Florida firefighter noticed that a used baby diaper was the only item that hadn't burned in a home that had been destroyed by fire. Figuring that whatever protected the diaper might be able to protect homes, he got together with a chemist and spent the next several years developing his idea.

He now has his product, which is basically a gel consisting of many layers of tiny sponges that absorb water. The gel is concentrated, and with a special attachment for your garden hose, can be sprayed onto your home, car, propane tank, bushes, or whatever you need to protect.

The gel is meant for emergency purposes, as it only lasts from a few hours to a day or more, depending on conditions. How long it lasts depends on factors such as the thickness of the gel coat applied, air temperature, and humidity.

I don't yet know anyone personally who has used it, but it does look very promising. At $150 (in 2002) for five quarts with a coverage of 500-700 square feet, it's not cheap, but if you do want to find out more, visit the website www.barricadegel.com.

Remember that no matter how well this diaper-inspired product may work, it is still important to make your home as "fire safe" as possible. You can do a lot to protect your home by modifying fuels around your structures, choosing fire-resistant building materials, and making sure you have a reliable water source in emergencies.

"Spring Cleaning" Checklist for Summer Fires

As we enter fire season each year, keep in mind that structures are lost to fires in California every fire season -- in 1999, the number was over 1500! CDF has a useful "Spring Cleaning" checklist of common-sense steps you and your family can take in and around your home to prepare for a fire.

A sampling of the topics covered in the checklist and precautionary steps suggested are given below. For a copy of the complete checklist, call 800-738-8733.

<u>Roof</u>
Remove dead branches overhanging your roof.
Remove branches within 10 feet of your chimney.
Clean dead leaves and needles from your roof and gutters.

<u>Landscape</u>
Create a "defensible space" and landscape with fire-resistant plants within 30' of structures.
For trees taller than 18 feet, prune lower branches within six feet of the ground.

<u>Fuel Sources</u>
Take note of what your fuel sources are, keep them 30 feet away from the house, and give them 10 feet of clearance. Common fuel sources include stacks of firewood, gas containers, and propane tanks.

<u>Emergency Water Supply</u>
Establish a cooperative emergency storage tank with neighbors or store at least 2,500 gallons on your property.
If your water comes from a well, consider an emergency generator to operate pumps during a power failure.

<u>Access</u>
Construct turnouts along narrow roads.
Trim and prune shrubs to the side and above the main access roads so that fire trucks can get through if need be.
If you are in the back woods, post your house number so firefighters can find your house.

<u>Outside</u>
Designate an emergency meeting place outside your home.
Practice emergency exit drills with your family.

<u>Construction</u>
Limit the size and number of windows in your home that face large areas of vegetation.
Install a fire-resistant roof.
Install dual-paned or triple-paned windows.

Wildfire and the Roof Over Your Head

It's not *if*, it's *when*. This is, or should be, the mantra of rural homeowners when it comes to wildfire. In fact, the disruption of the natural fire cycle (by fire suppression) tends to lull us into a false sense of security. The reality is that the choice to live in the woods should go hand-in-hand with planning for when the fire comes.

There are a number of things you can do to increase the likelihood that your home will survive a wildfire, beginning with the decision of where to build. Fire moves quickly on steep slopes and more slowly on gentle slopes. A home on a steep slope may give you a beautiful view but will be difficult if not impossible to protect.

Once your home is in place, remove flammable vegetation near the structure. This helps creates "defensible space" around your home. You can do this under a "fire exemption," which allows you to modify fuels within 150 feet of your residential structure. Within this area, all or some trees may be removed, and trees harvested under this kind of exemption may be sold, traded or bartered.

A third critical factor is the kind of roof you have. In the 1980s, the Pacific Southwest Research Station published a guide that underscored how much difference a fire-resistant roof can make. In the study, they found that homes with fire-resistant roofs were more than twice as likely to survive wildfire as homes with wood roofs. As the size of defensible space increased, fewer homes were lost, and the percentage of homes with fire-resistance roofs surviving the blaze reached 99%.

Removal of flammable vegetation	Homes lost with Wood Roofs	Homes lost with Fire-resistant Roofs
0- 30 feet	50%	24%
30- 80 feet	28%	5%
80-100 feet	15%	2%
100 + feet	15%	1%

For more information on fire exemptions or making your home more fire-resistant, call the Forest Stewardship Helpline, 800-738-8733.

Christmas Trees

Choosing Your Christmas Trees

For over 30 million US households, the family Christmas tree comes from a retail lot. If that's where you get your tree, remember that freshness is very important. When buying the tree, be sure the needles don't come off too easily. Most if not all of the (green) needles should stay on when you gently run a branch through your fingers or tap the tree on the ground.

But you may be lucky enough to be able cut your own tree, either on your property or elsewhere (permits from the Forest Service are available for a small fee). If you cut your own, try not to take a tree with a full crown that is open-grown. This would rob the forest of a tree that is already established and well on its way to becoming an important structural component of the forest. Instead, look for a tree that you might want to remove anyway if you were doing a thinning. It will be tough. Perhaps you'll resort to cutting two trees, each with a good crown only on one side, and binding them together!

If you want to know more about individual species, visit the website of the National Christmas Tree Association, at http://www. Realchristmastrees.org. This is an interesting site with lots of information, including tree selection, detailed information about more than a dozen of the most popular Christmas tree species, and how to care for your tree.

Caring for Your Christmas Tree

Over the winter holidays, lots of people will be bringing home their Christmas trees on the backs of pickups and on the roofs of cars. Others will be lucky enough to be able to cut a live tree from their own property and simply carry it into the house. Whatever the source of your tree, here are some tips for setting it up and taking care of it.

- Unless you have just cut your tree, make a new, fresh cut at the bottom of the main stem, about a quarter inch (or more) from the original cut. This will allow the tree to take up water freely.

- Water your tree. Check every day and add water as necessary. This will help keep the tree moist, which means you'll have fewer needles dropping off. Plenty of water will also keep the tree more fragrant.

- If you use a store-bought stand, a good rule of thumb is for it to be large enough to hold one quart of water for every inch of tree diameter. An average tree that is six feet tall has a diameter of about 4 inches, so you'd want a stand that could hold at least a gallon of water.

- Place the tree away from heat sources, including wood stoves, fireplaces, and space heaters. If possible, place the tree in a cool spot. This will cause it to use less water and will reduce the risk of fire.

- Place the tree away from doors where it might be at risk of being knocked over.

Following these simple steps will keep your home's tree, a symbol of life, fresh throughout this holiday season.

Water and Your Christmas Tree

If you have a real Christmas tree this year, you should be watering it every few days. If it's not using very much water, you may have forgotten to saw off ¼ to 1 inch of the trunk above the original cut after you brought the tree home. By making a new cut, you'll make it much easier for the tree to take up water. The principle is the same as recutting flowers to promote water uptake and the longevity. Each day your Christmas tree will use up to a gallon of water, depending on its species and size. But all this begs the question, where does all that water go?

Trees do something called "transpire," which is basically the evaporation of water from its leaves. (This is also called "evapo-transpiration.") In your living room, how much water your Christmas tree transpires depends on the size and species of the tree, how much foliage it has, as well as the amount of sunlight and temperature. In the forest, the same factors determine how much water is transpired, but there are a few additional factors, like wind and the availability of water in the soil.

Studies have been done to demonstrate how much variability there is in the amount of water trees transpire. One study found that every day birch trees transpired over 9 grams of water for each gram of weight of green leaves. In contrast, Douglas-fir transpired only a little over 1 gram per gram of green needles. Still, that's a lot of water.

So remember to water your Christmas tree regularly. And if it's not drinking properly, recut the stem. Treat your tree right, and it should stay green and vibrant until after New Year's.

Your Christmas Tree — A Little History

Is yours one of the estimated 36 million households in the US with a live Christmas tree? Here are a few bits of historical trivia about your tree.

The evergreen tree has long been a symbol of life. It was believed long ago in many countries that the fresh leaves and branches from evergreens (from both Christmas trees and wreaths) would protect a home from ghosts, sickness, and evil spirits.

Evergreen trees hung with red apples were used in the Middle Ages in the celebration of Adam and Eve, held December 24. There were known as "Paradise Trees."

The tradition of the indoor tree decorated with candles is said to have started with Martin Luther in Germany in the 1500s. Walking through the forest at night, he was struck by the beauty of the stars and wanted to share that little piece of magic with his children. So he decorated the tree with candles to represent those stars.

Tinsel came from Germany in the early 1600s. Real silver was used for many years.

A German company in the mid-1800s began making glass-bead garlands for Christmas trees. The idea quickly spread.

Electric Christmas tree lights originated in 1882, the brainchild of a colleague of Thomas Edison. Eight years later, they were being mass produced.

Today, there are even online trees, including games to make the trees light up.

May knowing a little more about your Christmas tree's history help you enjoy your tree and your holidays all the more!

Archaeological Sites -- Once a Site, Always a Site

One of my favorite aspects of working on management plans has always been looking for archaeological sites. There are some things about human nature that are constant, despite differences in culture, technology, or other aspects of our lives. For example, we tend to prefer spots that are cool in the summer or that have beautiful views.

And so in the field we find that archaeological sites are often found in predictable locations. Think of the places you like to camp, or the places you might choose to build a house. You are probably drawn to some of the same characteristics of a site the Native Americans were drawn to. Archaeologists sum this up with the simple phrase, "Once a site, always a site." Of course, the site today may have a house, a vineyard, or a town built upon it.

Since an archaeological report is a requirement for harvest plans in California, Registered Professional Foresters (RPFs) take a class on how to address archaeological resources out in the woods. After attending a recent class on locating and protecting archaeological sites, I received a nifty little brochure entitled "Protecting Archaeological Sites in California's Timberlands." This 8-page publication, designed for landowners and loggers, goes over the basics of where to look for sites, what to look for, requirements for a Timber Harvest Plan, and a lot more. It's a great resource for landowners as well as their foresters.

Where do you find sites? People need water, and we like to have flat areas on which we can easily move around and sleep. So most sites occur on flat areas near sources of fresh water that run year-round. A flat area above the confluence of two creeks is an especially likely spot.

Another very good spot to find a site is at the edge of a natural opening, like a meadow, where people can easily move from the sun in to the shade and back again. Here you might find pieces of chert or obsidian that were worked by men making arrowheads. Or you might find a flat stone upon which women used to grind acorns. On large boulders in or near watercourses, you just might be lucky enough to find a mortar or pestle. Keep your eyes open!

Connections in the Forest

If you look for relationships in the forest, you won't have to look far. Connections are many and varied, and they include everything from the trees overhead to the soil beneath your feet.

Some connections are easy to spot, like wildlife and trees: birds and trees, lizards and logs, or woodpeckers and snags. Others are readily seen if you think to look for them, for example wildlife, wood and water: you might see fish living in a deep pool scoured out by water that falls over a downed log in the stream. Still other connections are so subtle or difficult to discover that you never would have guessed they existed. One good example of this is something called something called "mycorrhizal associations."

 "Mycorrhizae" are fungi that help plants take up nutrients and even water. This "association" between the fungi and the roots of the plants is a symbiotic one, meaning that it is good for the plants and good for the fungi.

The mychorrizae fungi actually grow on the roots, but this does not harm the roots at all. It effectively gives the root system more surface area so that it can be more efficient. Exactly how it works is not entirely understood, but the results are clear. In addition to helping in the taking up of water and nutrients, mychorrizae help plants increase their resistance to high soil temperatures, toxins, and even pathogens that would harm the plant. It is said that mychorrizae are so important for pines that you don't find pines without them.

All this is happening silently and tirelessly as you walk through the woods. It is interesting to think about what other connections we never think about that are under our feet, above our heads, or right before our eyes.

Fall Colors

Each year as the poison oak leaves turn red and the bigleaf maple leaves turn yellow we marvel at the beauty of the fall colors. The poet in us may be content to know that Jack Frost is at it again, but the scientist in us knows there is more to the story.

In fact, the pigments that create the glorious fall colors are there in the leaves during the spring and summer. During those seasons, the tree is busy making food for itself through photosynthesis. Chlorophyll is the large molecule that makes photosynthesis possible by absorbing light. It is also a pigment that gives a leaf its green color. In all but a few species, the green chlorophyll prevents us from seeing xanthophylls (yellows) and carotenoids (reds, oranges and yellows).

With autumn come shorter days, cooler weather, and less intense sunlight. The change in weather signals the trees to stop making food. As the chlorophyll in the leaf breaks down, we begin to see the other colors that have been there all along but that were masked by the green of the chlorophyll.

You may have noticed that the most striking colors come when days are warm and sunny, followed by nights that are cool but not freezing. (Nighttime lows under 45 degrees are ideal, but freezing weather causes the leaves to wither quickly and fall to the ground.) Warm daytime temperatures allow for sugar production, and cool nights prevent the sugars from moving out of the leaves. The sugars trapped in the leaves produce a red pigment. Fewer of these sugars are produced when the fall weather is overcast, and they move more easily out of the leaves when the nights are warm, resulting in less intense colors.

So when autumn comes, be sure to wish Jack Frost warm sunny days and cool nights so that he can excel in his handiwork that we so admire each year.

Energy and The World's Best Solar Collectors

Increases in the price of electricity in the last few years have had people looking for ways to conserve energy. One likely upshot is that people will begin to look more seriously at renewable energy sources in order to reduce their dependence on expensive electricity delivered through the grid. One important renewable energy source not to be overlooked is wood. Trees are the best, most efficient, not to mention least expensive, solar collectors we have.

The most intuitive use for wood in terms of energy is to heat your home. When you heat with wood, conventional wisdom says that it warms you four times---first when you gather the wood, second when you transport it from the woods to your home, third when you carry it into the house, and finally when you burn it.

We also use wood to build our homes and structures. Apart from benefits of seismic stability and the aesthetic "feel" of wood, this makes good energy sense. The energy consumed to create and transport a steel stud, for example, to your homebuilding site is much greater than that needed to get a wood stud there.

You would think that we can't use wood to power our computers or the lights in your living room, but we certainly can. There are generation plants that run on something called "biomass," which is a fancy word for organic material like wood, yard waste, tree trimmings, etc. Small-diameter trees that are too small to be cut into sawlogs can be harvested and fed into a biomass plant, generating electricity. California has biomass plants in place already, which are listed on the website of the

California Biomass Energy Alliance at http://www.calbiomass.org. According to that site, the burning of wood in biomass plants produces only 3% of the pollution of open burning out in the woods.

In addition to large biomass plants, work is being done on "micro-biomass" generation in order to produce power on a smaller scale, under couple of hundred kilowatts.

Biomass-based energy generation may well be a technology whose time has come. Even state assemblyman Fred Keeley, who authored a bill to ban clearcutting in the state, indicated at a forestry meeting that he thought the idea of turning biomass from the woods into energy was a good suggestion and ought to be further pursued.

Our Nation's Tragedy and Our Interconnectedness

On Tuesday, September 11th at 8:00 am EDT, I boarded a plane to return home to San Francisco via Atlanta. Flying over the suburbs of Chicago, I was struck by the many buildings, cars, and ribbons of road amidst a vast urban forest and the obvious interconnectedness of it all. I marveled that we could ever imagine ourselves apart from the ecosystem.

Two hours later, we were circling the Atlanta airport. When the plane finally landed, the pilot announced that the entire country's airspace had been shut down. I wondered what on earth was going on—were we at war? We taxied from gate to gate, searching for a place to deplane. Finally the pilot shut down the engines and gave the OK to use cell phones.

As people began calling out, snippets of conversation floated in the air. "Oh, my God. Oh, my God!" "The World Trade Center? Fifty thousand people work there!" "I have friends in the Pentagon." Word quickly spread that several planes had been hijacked and crashed. Someone said another hijacked plane was going to be shot down. Passengers called home to let family know they were safe and on the ground. A man made calls for other passengers to let loved ones know they were OK. A businessman called his office to cancel meetings. A sailor translated what he knew to a Hispanic woman who didn't speak English. I quietly recited some prayers, with a heart full of alarm and grief and with eyes irresistibly drawn to the nearby planes that had not been the instruments of that morning's attacks.

As we deplaned two hours later, we caught glimpses of the TV news. Surreal glimpses of an impossible New York skyline. But it would be hours before we knew the full scope of what had happened. From a taxicab I read the ominous sign, "National Emergency. All Atlanta airports closed."

It was impossible to fully absorb the news that afternoon. Oddly, I was reminded of seeing the Grand Canyon for the first time. Its enormity made it seem unreal, like a postcard. It took time to take in its awesome scope. Likewise it will take time to understand the magnitude of this tragedy.

Days later I returned to the Atlanta airport, longing to just get home. There was a wordless anxiety at the gate as the flight was delayed again and again. When the pilots at last boarded the aircraft, the passengers applauded.

As life goes on, we are now changed and changing as we struggle to understand and respond to this crisis. We are a great people, and we do what we set our minds to do. We have been working hard to understand our interconnectedness to the forest. May we now work even harder to remember and nurture our interconnectedness to each other as human beings.

Stories from the Woods

"Mousing" Owls

At a session of the Forestry Institute for Teachers in Humboldt County a few years ago, our group of 40 was treated to the thrilling experience of seeing a couple of spotted owls up close and personal, courtesy of Simpson Timber. Several Simpson wildlife biologists spent the afternoon with us, looking at and talking about various wildlife species, including the spotted owl.

Foresters and wildlife biologists find owls by going out, generally at night, and hooting the spotted owl's special hoot. Since owls are territorial, and this hoot signifies to a resident owl that another owl is moving in to its territory, the resident owl will come over to check things out.

Soon, however, the owl figures out that the call is that of the forester or wildlife biologist. Unless that person "mouses" (feeds mice to) the owl, the bird loses interest and will no longer respond to the call. That makes it virtually impossible to determine survival and nesting status of the owls, so mousing has become accepted protocol.

These owls were expecting mice, and they were not in the least bit shy. Two of them, a pair, flew right over to the side of the road when our big yellow school bus pulled over. We got off the bus and congregated in the road while the wildlife biologists found a stick and brought out the mice. The owls, perched in second-growth Douglas-fir, waited patiently while the wildlife biologist talked to us about how they find and study the owls.

Then it was snack time for the owls. Two teachers took turns holding the 3-foot stick while the wildlife biologist put a live mouse on the end of the stick. Immediately both two owls flew over in a race to see who could get to the stick, and their snack, first. The one nearer the stick flew over the heads of the teachers between its perch and the stick, swooped down, expertly snatched the mouse, and returned to the Douglas-fir branch to eat the mouse. While that owl was feeding, another teacher eagerly volunteered to hold the stick for the next mouse.

Each owl was rewarded with a feeding, and each teacher was rewarded with a memory that will last a lifetime.

The Storrie of a Fire

In August of 2000, I was driving in the Sierras along the beautiful North Fork of the Feather River to a summer training camp for teachers. A helicopter caught my eye, and then an air tanker. When I saw a thin trail of smoke ahead, it all added up to a wildfire. Recognizing this as a rare opportunity to watch the firefighters in action, I pulled over to the side of the road behind another car. It was 2:30 in the afternoon on August 17 in a little place called Storrie.

There wasn't very much smoke, and the fire could not have been more than 1 or 2 acres in size. Over the course of the next half-hour, three air tankers dropped five loads of fire retardant. The helicopter dropped water more times than I could keep track of, as it was dipping out of the Feather River and had a turn-around time of only 2-3 minutes. Two Forest Service Hot Shot (firefighting) crews arrived and scurried up the steep slope to begin their work.

The wind was picking up, and it wasn't clear if all of these efforts would be able to contain the fire or not. The unbroken, dense field of green treetops looked like a sea of fuel for a hungry fire. Running late and hoping for the best, I decided to leave the scene and head up to camp.

That evening from camp we saw the great plumes of smoke. The fire had escaped. Teachers who had been out on a field trip that day reported that ash had fallen down upon them. It gave them a new appreciation for the links between a hands-off forest management approach, the accumulation of fuels, and risk of catastrophic wildfire that they had been hearing about all week. We were fortunate that the camp where we were staying was not threatened.

The next morning, another forester arrived at the camp with an update on the fire. He had been the driver of the car stopped in front of me the previous day. He had stayed to watch the firefighting efforts until the highway patrol ran him off at 5 pm. By that time, the fire, which had started at 2:15 pm, was 2,000 acres in size.

The Storrie Fire was not contained until several weeks later. It burned approximately 47,000 acres.

What do we want our forests to look like in 50 years? In 100 years? Will the things we are and aren't doing now get us there?

Resources for Landowners

Books

The Dictionary of Forestry – John Helms, editor, The Society of American Foresters, 1998. This is an excellent dictionary of a wide variety of forestry terms from "abiotic" to "zygote." Available from www.safnet.org.

Forest Owners' Guide to the Federal Income Tax – Internal Revenue Service, publication 718, 2001. Available through the Southern Research Station Publications website at http://www.srs.fs.usda.gov/pubs/viewpub.jsp?index=2207.

Handbook for Forest and Ranch Roads – William Weaver and Danny Hagans, Mendocino County Resource Conservation District, 1994. This is a superb resource for all your questions about building and maintaining roads. Very readable with lots of useful pictures and diagrams. Available from the Mendocino County RCD at 707-468-9223.

Pamphlets

A Property Owner's Guide to Reducing Wildfire Threat – University of California Cooperative Extension. Defensible space and management of vegetation adjacent to homes are discussed. Available from http://anrcatalog.ucdavis.edu, (530) 757-8930, or the Forestry Helpline.

Protecting Archaeological Sites in California's Timberlands – Available from CDF Archaeology or from the Forestry Helpline.

Thinning: An Introduction to a Timber Management Tool – Pacific Northwest Cooperative Extension, 1979. An oldie but goodie, this 10-page booklet is an excellent introduction to thinning and the reasons to do so. The booklet is clearly explains fundamental concepts so that the lay person can understand them. Available through the Forest Stewardship Helpline at 800-738-8733.

Other

The Forest Stewardship Helpline – Staffed by a Registered Professional Forester, this toll-free number was established under the federal Forest Stewardship Program to help landowners with their questions. Call 800-738-8733.

The Forestland Steward Newsletter –This outstanding publication of the Forest Stewardship Program has temporarily been suspended. If you are a forest landowner in California, call the Forest Stewardship Helpline (800-738-8733) to get your name on the list to receive the publication when printing resumes.

Forest Stewardship Series –This is a fabulous series of 24 publications addressing issues of interest to forest landowners, from fire and roads to taxation. 256 pages in total, available online. Published by the University of California, 2007. http://anrcatalog.ucdavis.edu/Forestry/8323.aspx